W9-AVT-061

UNDER EVERY ROOF

UNDER EVERY ROOF

A KIDS' STYLE AND FIELD GUIDE TO THE ARCHITECTURE OF AMERICAN HOUSES

Patricia Brown Glenn
Illustrated by Joe Stites

Preservation Press

John Wiley & Sons, Inc.
New York Chichester Brisbane Toronto Singapore

Published by John Wiley & Sons, Inc.

Library of Congress Cataloging in Publication Data
Glenn, Patricia Brown, 1953-
Under every roof: a kids' style and field guide to the
architecture of American houses / Patricia Brown Glenn;
illustrated by Joe Stites.
p. cm.
Includes bibliographical references.
Summary: A history and description of American house styles from
colonial times through the present.
ISBN 0-471-14428-2
1. Architecture, Domestic – United States – Juvenile literature.
[1. Architecture, Domestic. 2. Dwellings.] I. Stites, Joe, ill.
II. Title.
NA7205.G54 1993
728'.0973 – dc20 93-7627
AC

5 4 3 2

Designed and typeset by Garruba - Dennis, Washington, D.C.
Printed by Tien Wah Press, Singapore

DEDICATION

This book is dedicated to S. Lane Faison, Jr., Amos Lawrence Professor of Art, Emeritus, Williams College, and Director of Williams College Art Museum, Emeritus, who taught me how to see what I was looking at. And to my husband, Christopher, who never stops believing in me.

CONTENTS

INTRODUCTION

Homes across America, in big cities, in small towns, and out in the country, are as different and as alike as the people who live in them. They provide us with shelter and keep us warm, cool, dry, and safe through the changing seasons.

We all have neighbors. Some live next door, others live in the upstairs apartment, and still others live down the road. The neighbors' houses, for the most part, are pretty much like ours. Together our homes make up the blocks, neighborhoods, and communities that are our towns. So the character of our towns is defined by the homes that we live in.

Let's stop for a minute and think: do our house and our neighborhood look different from houses and neighborhoods in other parts of the country? Why, for instance, do Southern homes always have a porch? Why is the New England Saltbox just a plain gray rectangle with a steep roof that's longer in back than in front? What about the tall New York Brownstones that stand side by side on such narrow lots or the Wyoming Ranch House and all its outbuildings spread out over acres and acres of land? The way a home looks is often determined by the climate and geography of its location.

Have you ever noticed that some houses are very decorative, with fancy carved woodwork, marble columns, or intricate brick work, while others are quite plain and ordinary? Some of these differences have to do with personal taste and what people find attractive or pleasing. Some people have summer and winter residences that are big enough to be hotels, while others live in a cozy bungalow year round. Some people live in homes that can be hooked up to their car and driven away at any time. Some people live on the water in a houseboat. Can you imagine someone who might prefer a home shaped like a shoe? What about a house shaped like a dome that you can construct yourself out of aluminum, Plexiglas, vinyl, or paperboard?

Economics – what people can afford – determines the way a house will look. Lifestyle is an important part of this equation, too.

Sometimes the way a house looks evolves out of a certain tradition. Early immigrants to America adapted their traditional ways of building to suit the weather, the lay of the land, their household needs, and what they could build with local materials and techniques. Over time, vernacular housing–architecture that is characteristic of a particular people and place–has become so much a part of our architectural heritage that much of the housing in our country fits that description. People in all parts of the United States have created houses that speak about their culture, what they find beautiful, and the patterns of their family life. The German stone houses of Pennsylvania or the Dutch brick homes of New York are examples of vernacular housing.

Once we understand the reasons houses look the way they do, we can consider the way houses look–their style. Houses built in a certain place and at a certain time period often have similar characteristics. The best example of a particular style–for example, the Prairie Style Robie House in Chicago–is often architect-designed and referred to as "High Style" architecture because of the clarity of its design. Architects who are less famous or contractor-builders often borrow ideas from a specific style then change them slightly by using different materials or by altering the size or the floor plan. Frequently styles overlap, and a house may have more than one design influence: for instance, a Prairie Style house with Stick Style detailing. These variations reflect the taste and the building customs of different regions. Most of the houses in America fit this description.

Today many architects are deeply concerned about energy-efficient housing, providing quality living places for the homeless, and solving the housing needs of a growing population here and abroad. In each of these cases, function will determine not only the best style for each structure, but which materials and which location will be the most suitable.

This brings us to the final and most personal part of this book: your house. Can you figure out why it looks the way it does? What kind of roof does it have, and why? What materials is it made of? How does it keep you warm or cool? What style is it? The Style Guide in Part II and the Field Survey in Part III will help you answer some of these questions; the rest you can discover in the pages that follow, in conversations with family members and neighbors, by learning about your community, and, most important, by looking around you. What is really happening under your roof? Let's turn the page and find out.

PART ONE

WHY HOUSES LOOK THE WAY THEY DO

CHOOSING YOUR LOCATION

The location or site of a house is the first and perhaps most important influence on its design. The pioneers knew that the best place for a homestead would have access to water, plenty of timber, and a supply of game for food. Neighbors close enough for company on the lonely prairie and for help in the event of trouble were certainly desirable. If towns were nearby, necessary supplies could be bought, and trading could take place close to home.

By contrast, in larger cities like New York or San Francisco, where space was limited and land was expensive, town houses and apartments were constructed on narrow lots facing the street. A party wall, or shared wall between two properties, separated the buildings from one another. Large windows in front and in back of the house allowed for a nice breeze, and front steps provided a pleasant place to socialize or to keep cool.

Today a bulldozer can level any site and prepare it for construction. The temperature in our houses can be controlled for comfort, and indoor plumbing and electricity make it possible for us to live wherever we choose. Some architects, however, are sensitive to the lay of the land when they build their houses and look to examples from the past to guide them.

Site selection was clearly a major factor in the settlement near Laramie, Wyoming, of the nearly 5,000-acre Boswell Ranch: the location is ideal for raising cattle. The Big Laramie River meanders through this ranch land, which is bordered to the east by the Rocky Mountains and to the west by the pine-covered Medicine Bow Range. Grass and sage cover the hillsides, and deer and elk roam the wooded areas. At the turn of the century, the Union Pacific railheads were nearby, making it convenient to ship cattle to market.

The log ranch house of 1873 and the original outbuildings from later in the 19th century are handmade structures. Their beauty is in the simplicity of their design and the grandeur of their setting against the big sky and rugged landscape of Wyoming.

CLIMATE

Before air conditioning and central heating, American houses were designed to keep the interior warm in winter and cool in summer, to shed the weight of snow, and to offer shelter from the rain. It makes sense that in different climates house shapes will vary either to protect from the weather or to take advantage of it.

The adobe block house or pueblo, first built in the 1500s, was well suited to the hot, dry climate of New Mexico, Arizona, and Texas. Developed from Spanish and Native American traditions, these houses had flat roofs and thick walls made of adobe or sun-baked clay blocks. They were built around a central courtyard. The adobe walls soaked up the desert sun during the day and enabled the house to stay warm at night. The interior courtyard was sheltered from the wind and offered a pleasant retreat morning or evening. Equally important, the adobe walls became a fortress during enemy attacks. For protection the family retreated to the inner courtyard, which could be closed off by a heavy wooden door.

A Louisiana plantation house like Oak Alley depends on wide galleries or verandas that wrap around the exterior to shield it from the heat. The wide hip roof shades the interior of the house as well as the outdoor porches that provide additional living space. Oversized windows, especially on the second floor where the bedrooms are, catch the breeze. Some houses even have a sleeping porch located upstairs that is screened in on three sides. A rooftop pavilion or belvedere has windows that open in summer to allow rising heat to escape.

Oak Alley - Plantation House - Louisiana

In more recent times, the A-Frame has become the ideal vacation home. The steep gable roof extends almost to the ground on two sides, doubling as walls and, in mountainous areas, quickly sloughing off snow. A glass wall on the south lets in warmth and sunlight, and the cozy floor plan, centered on the living room fireplace, creates an inviting retreat for tired skiers. The exterior deck becomes the ideal outdoor living space in summer; the sliding glass doors let in cool breezes.

The American Indians, like the early settlers, depended on the land to provide them with the raw materials necessary for shelter and food. The homes of the Indians varied from region to region, as did the building materials they used to construct them. Some tribes lived in communal housing much like a modern apartment complex, while others stayed with just their own family in a small hut or tepee. But regardless of the social or family traditions within each group or their style preferences, the Indian people were resourceful, imaginative builders who used nature's bounty to develop their architecture and to build their communities. A sampling of some different dwellings from around the country follows.

Popular with Plains and Northwest Indians, the Earth Lodge was a deep pit dug out of the ground and covered over with branches and mud. These grassy or snow-covered mounds were detectable only by the column of smoke rising in the air. Later the structures became more permanent, using a wooden, cone-shaped frame with an exterior made of thick willow brush and a roof of thatched grass or pine needles under a six-inch layer of sod. They were entered through an earth-covered tunnel, with doorways made of buffalo skins. The lodges were quite roomy, measuring 8 feet deep and as much as 40 feet across. A fireplace at the center provided heat, and light came in through the "smoke hole" in the roof. The Earth Lodge or "Pit House" was home to as many as 40 people, all from the same family.

THE EARTH LODGE

The pueblos of the Anasazi Indians in Mesa Verde, Colorado, are an excellent example of the type of shelter developed by the Southwest Indians. Seemingly carved from the sandstone cliffs, these adobe and stone villages gave the Indians a good position from which to protect themselves. Their homes were entered by ladders that led to a hole in the roof and could be quickly retracted in the event of an attack. The pueblos were grouped like an apartment complex, with units stacked one on top of another. The one-room home was private, functional, and simple, serving the family as a kitchen by day and a bedroom at night.

THE CLIFF PALACE DWELLING
MESA VERDE NATIONAL PARK - COLORADO
1220

The cone-shaped tepee was ideally suited to the nomadic, buffalo-hunting Plains Indians. Quickly constructed of natural materials, the tepee was functional, light in weight, and easy to carry. The steep sides shed winter snow and rain, but they could also be lifted to ventilate the tepee in hot weather. Smoke from the interior fire escaped through flaps at the top.

Women were responsible for building these simple tents. They arranged saplings in a cone shape and covered them with tanned and sewn buffalo hides. Men decorated the finished tepee by painting on the outside skins scenes praising the buffalo, telling of successful wars, or showing their thankfulness to the gods.

A BASIC TEPEE

The Indians of Southeast Alaska constructed wooden plank clan houses such as the reconstructed Totem Bight house in Ketchikan, Alaska. The low, oval entrance opened into a single large room with a central square fire pit. Families lived on the planked platform surrounding the fire.

THE CLAN HOUSE

Although we often think of the log cabin as the typical pioneer dwelling, homes on the frontier were often built of soil. The earliest example, the Dugout, has much in common with the Indian Earth Lodge. Both were carved out of the ground and covered by a grass roof. The construction made it difficult to spot these houses on the open prairie. A more sophisticated soil house was known as the Soddie. It was quite common in central Nebraska, where other building materials were unavailable. "Nebraska Marble" was the fancy-sounding name given to the sod bricks cut from the earth that were used to form the walls of these structures. Doorways and windows were usually framed with wood, and the whole house was covered with a hip roof, a low, tent-shaped roof with sloping sides and ends. Although the Soddie was comfortable year round and economical to construct, it was hard to keep clean and often overrun with insects.

THE SOD ON THIS HOUSE IS PROTECTED BY A COAT OF PLASTER AND CONCRETE.

WILLIAM R. DOUSE HOUSE
CUSTER CO., NEBRASKA - 1900

Sod houses were common in Nebraska, but the William R. Douse House near Comstock is the only such structure in the state being preserved as a representative of this type. Built in 1900, the original single-story house was covered by a shingled hip roof and had an attached porch with a shed roof. The L-shaped three-room plan included a large room that was a combination hall and kitchen, a smaller room that served as dining room and parlor, and a tiny room in the rear corner. Stairs led up to an unfinished attic area. The interior walls were plastered. Exterior wall coverings are of two types: an early surface made of clay, straw, and hog's-hair plaster, and a concrete coating applied in 1935 to stabilize the walls and protect them from the weather. The home was enlarged in 1924, but the original structure was not altered. A tornado leveled the surrounding outbuildings, including a barn, a chicken coop, a hog house, and a windmill.

Of all the materials used in house building, wood is certainly the most popular. It is versatile enough to adapt to almost any design: the rough-cut logs of the Pioneer cabin, supporting post and lintel construction, beautifully grained and polished interior paneling, or the carved and turned decoration of a Victorian house.

Each type of wood – and there are many – has its own special properties that make it the right choice for different architectural projects. Victorian Queen Anne scrollwork was often cut from California redwood because it did not splinter and it was durable, strong, and cheap. The Southern cypress is perfect for the damp climate of Louisiana because it is water resistant and does not permit rot. The Indians of the Northeast framed their wigwams with flexible sycamore saplings and covered them with a birch bark roof and cedar shingles to shed rain and snow. In the Midwest, oak has been favored for its strength and particularly for its beauty when it is highly polished for interior use in flooring and banisters.

The colonial house of Jethro Coffin in Nantucket, Massachusetts, has walls made of shake shingles that are hand split from logs. These shakes protected the house from the cold New England winter gales. On the north side of the house the sloping roof, also covered with hand-split shingles, reaches almost to the ground, giving additional protection against bad weather.

JETHRO COFFIN HOUSE
NANTUCKET MASS. - LATE 1600s

SHINGLES

Each material has its own special look. Dutch and English brick masons decorated the gable end of their houses by laying the bricks in a design. The Abraham Yates House in Schenectady, New York, dates from the early 1700s. The brick of this house is laid in zigzag diamonds called mousetoothing or tumbling. The initials of the builders or owners and the dates of construction are often recorded in the gable, too. Another feature was decorative iron "anchors" that secure the bricks to the wall, keeping them from shifting.

The early German stone houses in Pennsylvania made clever use of their building material to provide a comfortable and safe retreat. The steep gable roof, the two-foot thick stone walls, and the small windows kept the house cool, warm, and dry from season to season. When possible, the house was built over a stream to provide indoor refrigeration and running water. Because stone resists water damage, it allowed for this ingenious convenience. The Hans Herr House, built in 1719, is a fine example of this building type. It was the first German settlement in Lancaster County, Pennsylvania. The stone basement of this house may have been designed to offer the family shelter from possible attack. Windows measuring 30 inches wide on the inside narrow to 6 inches wide on the outside – just large enough to support a rifle.

JOHN DICKINSON HOUSE
ALLOWAY VICINITY
NEW JERSEY
1754

We have seen that the shape of a house had a lot to do with location, climate, and building materials. This is especially true in houses built before the invention of modern heating and cooling systems. Of course, there are other reasons why a house looks as it does – style, personal taste, and economics.

We can tell so much just by looking at a house. The outline of the roof, the ways in which the walls meet, the direction and the intersection of the lines all contribute to the design of the whole building. Materials and their texture can make the house warm and inviting or cold and distant. The way these elements are put together gives the house its character.

When you look at a house, consider: is it basically square, rectangular, diamond shaped, or rounded? A combination of these? Are the lines straight, zigzag, or curved? Is the roof conical, sloping, or flat? What is the house made of? How do those materials make you feel?

PHILIP JOHNSON'S "GLASS HOUSE"
NEW CANAAN, CONNECTICUT
1949

Monticello, the late 18th-century home designed and lived in by President Thomas Jefferson, has a complex and varied profile. The home is interesting to look at from any angle because Jefferson used so many different shapes and lines.

By contrast, the glass house designed by Philip Johnson couldn't be more austere. This simple rectangular box, designed in 1949, is so thoroughly transparent that we see both inside and outside at the same time. Nature and interior furnishings become a part of the total look.

Orson Squire Fowler designed and built an octagonal house for himself in the 1850s. He liked the eight-sided plan so much that, in his book called *The Octagon House: A Home for All*, he recommended that everyone live in an Octagon House. On the top of the building he designed a belvedere, a small cupola that provided natural light and helped fresh air to circulate throughout the house. The rooms were arranged around a central core that extended from the ground floor up to the roof. Balconies encircled the house, and windows, shaded by balcony roofs, caught the summer breezes. Central heating, gas lights, and indoor plumbing with running water and flush toilets were parts of Fowler's advanced design – modern for its time and unusual under one roof. Unfortunately, Fowler's house no longer stands, but the influence of his octagon plan was far reaching.

Look closely at this floor plan for an Octagon House. Can you find the stairs? The windows? The closets? Compare the shapes of the rooms in the Octagon House with the rooms in your house. How many rooms are square? How many are rectangles? How many are pie-shaped? The way a house looks on the outside certainly determines what the house will look like on the inside.

LONGWOOD, "NUTT'S FOLLY", NATCHEZ, MISSISSIPPI – 1860

Longwood, or "Nutt's Folly," in Natchez, Mississippi, is a wonderful example of an Octagon House. It was designed in 1860 by architect Samuel Sloan for Dr. Halles Nutt. The five-story mansion has a large onion dome and was the grandest and most ornate Octagon House in the country. The outbreak of the Civil War prevented the house from being completed.

Anyone who has seen the "Painted Ladies" of San Francisco knows first hand the importance of color to architectural design. Most of these 28,000 Victorian row houses were built between the mid-1800s and 1915. The 1906 earthquake and fire destroyed thousands of these houses, and many more were neglected or seriously altered during the world wars. In the 1960s and 1970s, with the birth of the historic preservation movement, these old buildings began to be restored to the wonderful and colorful homes they were meant to be.

Constructed on a narrow (25-foot) lot, the Victorian row house depended on the large central bay window for light and air. Only the facade was exposed to the street, and it was the principal surface available for decoration. It was bedecked with pediments, columns, scrolls, sunbursts, acanthus leaves, rosettes, brackets, balusters, faces, and more, all made out of carved, shaped, turned, and stamped redwood. Originally painted white with green shutters, these homes were gradually coated in rich colors like vermilion, sage, mustard, olive, maroon, terra cotta, mauve, and Venetian red. Painters began to experiment with different colors to make the trim and details stand out. They even allowed each floor to have its own color. Sometimes as many as 11 colors appeared on one house! By the turn of the century, advances in printing allowed paint companies to produce and distribute inexpensive paint sample cards and colored prints of houses. Illustrated guides on how and where paint could be applied encouraged homeowners to buy and use these products. Restoration of these houses saved a San Francisco legacy, provided quality housing, and employed skilled artisans.

ALAMO SQUARE NEIGHBORHOOD- SAN FRANCISCO CALIFORNIA LATE 1800s

Color has always been used to highlight interior and exterior spaces. Historic houses, for the most part, have been painted in white or in pale shades. Early New Englanders preferred natural woods, only occasionally painting their homes and barns red. Hot southern climates in the South and Southwest have preferred light colors, which reflect the sun away from the house, helping to keep it cool. The colonial plantation house, with its rows of columns supporting the roof, seems even more imposing and important when painted white. This same effect is achieved by the White House, which was originally whitewashed in 1797 to protect the exterior. The more recent International Style favors a stark white and glass exterior, while other modern designs limit their use of color primarily to interior spaces.

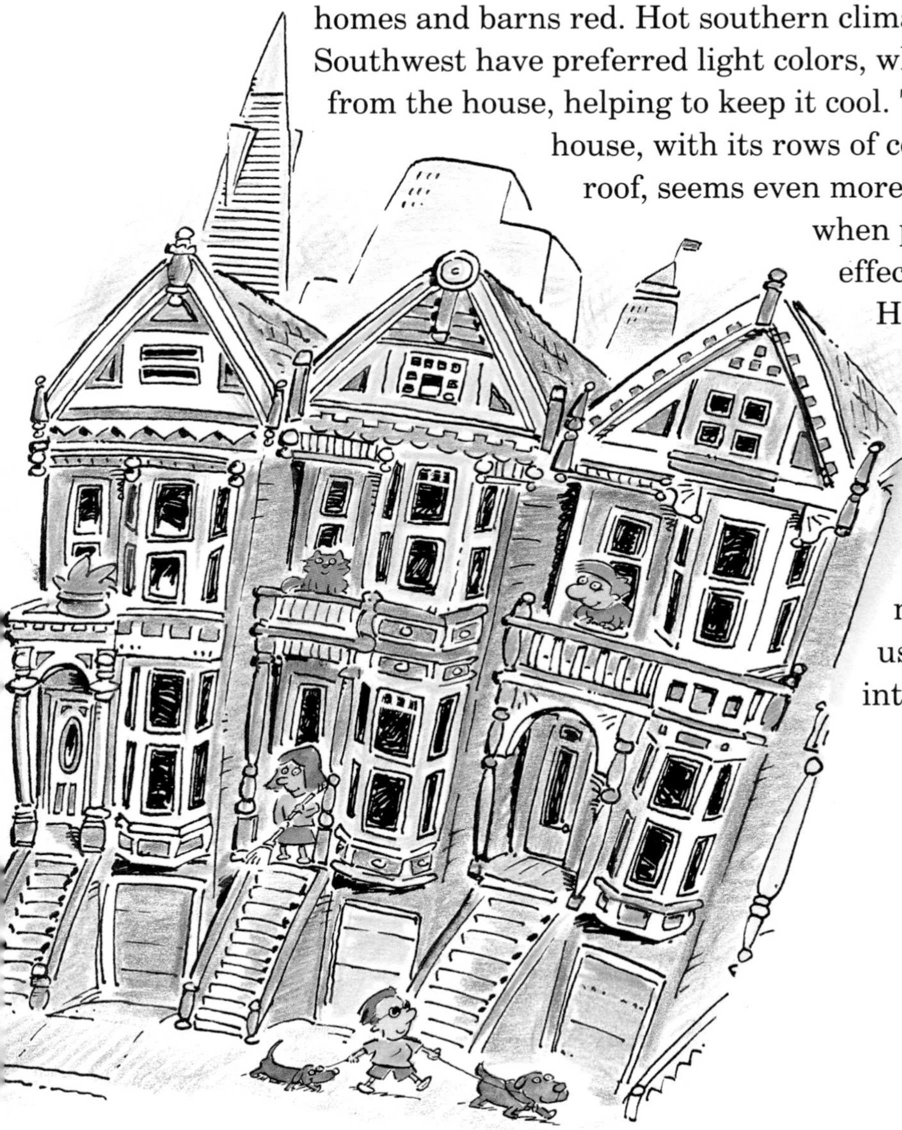

"POST CARD ROW"

Housing design over the past two centuries has depended in no small measure on the influence of architectural pattern books and mail order catalogues. *The Country Builder's Assistant* (1797) by Asher Benjamin is thought to be the first architectural plan book. True pattern books came on the scene in the 1830s. Architects and designers published them themselves in an effort to teach homeowners about style and good taste. The books included scenic views of residences, accompanying floor plans, and often interiors. *The Architecture of Country Homes* (1850), by Andrew Jackson Downing, was a particularly popular volume, and it was reprinted many times. Downing's house plans were economical and simple, but embellished with elaborate exterior architectural detailing.

Toward the end of the century, elevations or drawings of how the outside of the house would look and floor plans appeared regularly in popular magazines such as *Ladies Home Journal* and *Good Housekeeping*. The number of people reading the magazines increased, and the possibility of building and owning their own home became a greater reality for more Americans.

DOWNING'S "FRENCH ROOF HOUSE" FROM 1842 IS A PATTERN HOUSE

Yet another type of plan book, the manufacturer's mail-order catalogue, was introduced in the early 20th century. Catalogues offered not only house plans but also all the materials needed to construct them. Sears, Roebuck and Company quickly became the leader in this market by making available precut lumber, ready to be shipped and then assembled on delivery anywhere in the United States. Furthermore, Sears offered financing up to one hundred percent of the total cost of construction, a practice unheard of before this time. Sears offered approximately 80 different plans over the years. Options ranged from a quaint bungalow for as little as $629 to a handsome nine-room Dutch Colonial costing just under $5,000.

Homes built from pattern books and from mail order catalogues line the streets of neighborhoods across our country. They offered an affordable and fashionable way for more citizens to realize the American Dream of owning their own home. Today, specialty magazines and newspapers offer house plans for interested buyers. Prefabricated or easily assembled housing has been greatly improved, is available at reasonable prices, and is in great demand.

Personal Taste and Interior Decoration

A home usually reflects its owners' personal tastes. Mr. and Mrs. George Vanderbilt wanted the Biltmore estate and gardens to look like the castles of France. One thousand workers under the direction of architect Richard Morris Hunt labored for five years to build this country retreat. The Vanderbilts did not try to economize by using only local materials for their house; they could afford to pay for marble, tile, and crystal imported from Europe and rugs from the Orient. Rooms were filled with paintings and sculpture by famous artists, and rich tapestries covered the walls. Fresh flowers and plants from the Biltmore greenhouse were everywhere. And that was not all! The gardens, meadows, and roadways around the mansion were landscaped by Frederick Law Olmsted, the designer of Central Park in New York City. The Biltmore was a wonderful place to vacation and to entertain friends, but it was also a statement of the Vanderbilts' wealth and worldliness.

IMAGINE THE HIDE AND SEEK GAME YOU COULD HAVE HERE!!

Preserved as a historic house museum, Biltmore is open to visitors, allowing many people to appreciate its splendid furnishings and grounds and to learn about a different way of life.

BILTMORE ESTATE
ASHEVILLE, NORTH CAROLINA
1895

There may be a type of house that is special or unique to your city or geographic region. The mottled stone residences of Massachusetts are called Pudding Stone houses. In Missouri, Giraffe Stone houses are made from local spotted stone. Some early Missouri immigrants built yet another type of stone house and barn combination similar to dwellings they had left behind in Germany. Vernacular or folk architecture is the name given to houses that are found only in certain areas. Usually these buildings are not designed by an architect, but instead are built according to traditions handed down from generation to generation and from place to place.

HOME SWEET HOME

BARN SWEET BARN

WILLIAM PELSTER HOUSE
SOUTH HAVEN, MISSOURI
1860

William Pelster, his family, and his livestock all lived together in a housebarn in Missouri. All that was valuable to him was conveniently and safely located beneath one roof. He didn't even need to go out much to take care of his chores! The unpredictable and often harsh midwestern climate made this a good arrangement.

In the Northeast, the continuous house offered a different solution to the same problem. Here the house, the shed, and the barn are connected by corridors so that the farmer almost never needed to go outside in bad weather.

Unusual Houses and Their Names

SUNDAY HOUSE

Sometimes a house gets its name from the way it looks or from a special feature that makes it unique.

Not wanting to miss church on Sunday or trading at the Saturday market the day before, Texas ranchers and farmers living outside the city owned Sunday Houses. Built to be stayed in on weekends, these houses were just large enough for cooking a couple of meals, sleeping overnight, and hitching up a horse to the front porch post.

BALL HOUSE
SAN ANTONIO, TEXAS
KING WILLIAM HISTORIC DISTRICT
1868

Louisiana folklore tells how the Shotgun house got its name. All the rooms are lined up one behind the other, with all the passageways in a straight line. A sharpshooter with a rifle could stand at the front door and shoot a bullet straight through the house and out the rear door to kill a chicken in the backyard.

SHOTGUN HOUSE

IRISH CHANNEL HISTORIC DISTRICT
NEW ORLEANS, LOUISIANA
MID 1800s

In Alexandria, Virginia, a curious half house with a shed roof and a doorway and windows in the gable end facing the street is called a Flounder House. The side walls are windowless, so the house is named for the flounder, a fish that has eyes only on one side of its body. Local tradition suggests that these houses might have been intended as the rear end of a yet-to-be-built larger residence. For this reason they are often set back on lots and have no windows on the tallest side.

ALEXANDRIA HISTORIC DISTRICT
ALEXANDRIA, VIRGINIA
1824

The southern Dog Trot cabin took its name from the breezeway where the family hound often slept on hot summer nights. This cool passage separated the living room and bedroom on one side from the kitchen and dining room on the other. It also served as a main entrance for the house and as a handy storage spot for kitchen pans.

The gold and silver rush of the late 1800s brought laborers, lawyers, geologists, mule skinners, assayers, merchants, preachers, prospectors, and saloon keepers to small towns across the American West. Camps quickly sprang up around mining sites. Workers' cottages and cabins, boarding houses, and maybe a school or meeting housing were simple wood frame or log buildings. The supervisor's house was usually larger and fancier, often set apart from the miners' quarters. The towns were often abandoned when the rich mineral deposits thinned out; when the price for zinc, lead, copper, silver, or gold fell too low; or when a great calamity hurt the mining community. Tumble-down shacks, rusting mine works, and meandering streams are all that remain of these once-bustling ghost towns.

A ghost town is all that is left of the old Alta mining camp in the Colorado Rockies. Located 11,500 feet above sea level in the Silver Mountains, the mine had runs of close to 300 ounces of silver per ton during its hey day.

THE ALTA MINING CAMP TODAY IS A GHOST TOWN.

Telluride, Colorado, began as a mining camp in the late 1800s. The large amounts of silver and gold mined in the surrounding mountains soon drew many settlers, and the camp grew into a real town. By 1881 Telluride supported two newspapers and a commercial district complete with grocery and hardware stores, barber shop, stage office, hotels, livery stable, drug emporium, dry goods stores, and plenty of saloons and gambling houses. Four churches, a school, a courthouse, and a cemetery developed in short order. By the late 1890s the town had two banks, and its prosperity had earned it the nickname of "Town Without a Belly Ache."

Day laborers and workers lived in modest wooden houses away from the center of town. Wealthier citizens built quaint Victorian cottages with fanciful wooden trim or larger brick homes in Queen Anne style along busy Colorado Street. When the Rio Grande Southern Railroad came to Telluride in 1890, it linked this mountain town with Denver, Ridgeway, and, ultimately, Durango. Transporting the ore from the mines to market became much easier, and the population of the town soon swelled to nearly 5,000.

MAIN STREET – TELLURIDE, COLORADO

Telluride enjoyed great prosperity until the first decades of the 1900s, when mining profits diminished and strikes crippled productivity. By 1930 the banks had closed, and Telluride's population dwindled to 512. Today, because developers have planned carefully, Telluride has been reborn as an exciting winter ski resort and summer mountain retreat. The original character of the small western mining town has been maintained, safeguarding its special history and charm.

Is there an important house in your neighborhood? Is it special because it is old? Because of the person who lives there? Because of its architecture? Or because something significant happened there? A building that meets these standards can be listed in the National Register of Historic Places, our nation's honor roll of places worth saving. The National Register plaque on a building is the United States' way of saying "This architectural site has special meaning for all our citizens, and we want to preserve its history for future generations." If a building is listed in a local register, that means that its historical importance is only recognized in the particular city or town where it is located.

PAUL REVERE'S HOUSE
BOSTON, MASS. – 1680
(AS IT APPEARS TODAY)

American patriot Paul Revere lived in this house in Boston from 1770 to 1800. He is famous for warning the colonists in April of 1775 that the British were approaching. Henry Wadsworth Longfellow tells of this heroic deed in his poem "Paul Revere's Ride." Revere is also known as a fine artisan and silversmith.

INGALLS HOME
210 THIRD STREET
DeSMET, SOUTH DAKOTA
1887

This was the family homestead of Laura Ingalls Wilder, author of the famous Little House on the Prairie books. In her writings, Laura described the hardships and joys of pioneer life in Kansas, on the Minnesota frontier, and on the plains of South Dakota. Although Laura never actually lived here, she considered this house, built by "Pa," to be her home.

In 1927 Charles A. Lindbergh made the first nonstop flight across the Atlantic, from New York to Paris. He spent his boyhood summers on this Minnesota farm. The frame bungalow is decorated with turn-of-the-century furniture and contains Lindbergh family memorabilia.

Hawaii is the only state of the United States ever to have had resident royalty or royal palaces. King Kalākaua lived in `Iolani Palace in Honolulu from 1882 until his death in 1891. His sister, Queen Lili'uokalani, succeeded him and lived in the palace until the end of the Hawaiian monarchy in 1893. Designed by three different architects, the palace was spacious and richly decorated. It had private living quarters and special rooms for entertaining. From 1893 to 1969 `Iolani Palace was recognized as the capitol of the Republic, the Territory, and ultimately the State of Hawaii. Since that time the Friends of `Iolani Palace have restored and maintained the building as a house museum.

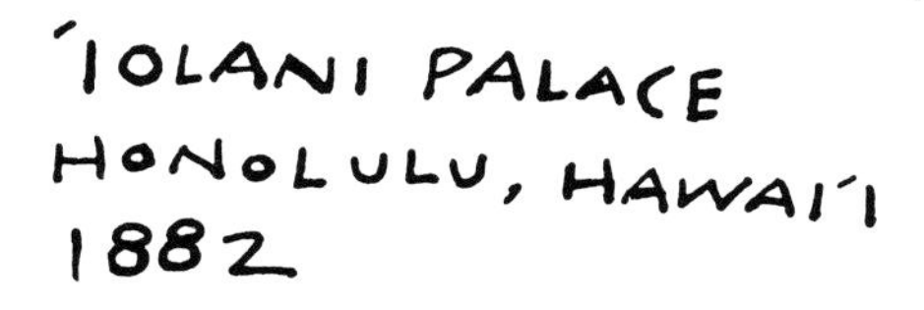

Political and Historical Importance

When George Washington envisioned the president's house in 1792, he saw a mansion that would be as imposing and as everlasting as the American people, spirit, and country. Though the White House has been altered and reconstructed many times during its history – after the British set fire to it during the War of 1812 and then during the administration of President Harry Truman, when it was completely gutted and rebuilt – it has remained America's first and most important public building.

Designed in 1791 by architect and builder James Hoban, the White House originally had 32 rooms and was located on a 10-acre piece of land. Today the building at 1600 Pennsylvania Avenue has 132 rooms, and the "President's Park" surrounding it has been enlarged to 18 acres. The White House, like our nation, has grown over the years. New presidents and their families, staffs, political agendas, and personal tastes and habits have required more space, more services, richer decorations, and many other changes. Through it all the White House has maintained its dignity and its sense of permanence.

The house is significant not only because the chief of state lives and works there, but also because it stands as a symbol of democracy to the American people. In this way the White House is a home for all, or, as Thomas Jefferson said, "the people's house."

The north portico, the principal entrance to the White House, has a triangular pediment supported by colossal Ionic columns. It resembles the early temples of Greece and Rome. Hoban and every architect after him borrowed from classical designs to remind us that our democratic form of government had its beginnings in these ancient civilizations.

The mansion stands three stories tall from the ground floor up, with three additional floors located underground. It measures 85 feet high and is 175 feet in length. The exterior is surfaced in buff-colored sandstone quarried in nearby Virginia. Because this material is very porous, the building was whitewashed for protection in 1797. It was called the President's House and the Executive Mansion until 1901, when Theodore Roosevelt officially dubbed it the "White House."

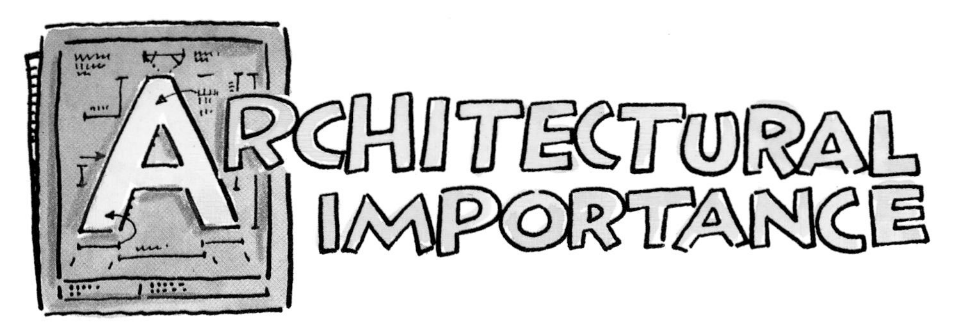

Sometimes a house design comes along that is so unusual, so new, and so right for the time and place that it signals an important trend in architecture. The Prairie Style developed by Frank Lloyd Wright in Chicago at the turn of the century was just such a design.

Wright thought of the house as a shelter that grew out of and was part of the landscape surrounding it. The organic mass of the Prairie Style house had long, low horizontal lines, echoing the flat Midwestern plains. This style broke from the more cubic classical traditions of ancient Greece and Rome that were popular at this time. Wright felt strongly that the Prairie house should be simple, beautiful, and above all functional.

Wright's strong feeling for form, structure, and simple materials goes back to the Froebel blocks he played with as a child. These colored geometric shapes, actually toys for school-age children, could be arranged in an endless number of patterns. When Wright designed houses, he used the blocks again and again to help him understand the relationship between empty space and solid walls. Wright preferred not to enclose rooms with four walls but to define them with partitions. Large areas of space gave the residents of the house greater flexibility to make a room suit many needs.

Wright was very interested in decorative art and interior furnishings, and he was fascinated with architectural ornament. These interests led him to make the house a complete work of art. He used complementary colors, shapes, materials, and detailing both inside and outside. Because he was concerned about the residence as a whole, he designed fabrics for upholstery, light fixtures, stained glass windows, and furniture.

STAINED GLASS CASEMENT WINDOWS

The appeal of the Prairie Style was enormous. When the style reached its peak of popularity in 1905, pattern books and popular magazines inspired variations throughout the Midwest and other regions of the United States.

During the more than 70 years of his career, Frank Lloyd Wright contributed many new ideas to American architecture. He will always be thought of as one of our country's most outstanding designers.

ECONOMICS

Around the turn of the 20th century, home ownership became an important issue for many Americans. A simple, affordable, attractive house was what people wanted – one that would be just right for their lifestyle no matter where they lived. The bungalow, introduced in California, offered the perfect solution – one to two stories tall with wide overhanging roofs and a broad front porch. It could be built in a variety of styles and materials to suit every taste and pocketbook.

In no time neighborhoods throughout the nation were filled with bungalows. Bungalow floor plans and styles, like those for the Victorian pattern-book house, could be selected directly from monthly journals, catalogues, and plan books. Architects again were unnecessary because contractor-builders could erect houses following a published blueprint. Often the builders put up the houses on speculation – built them, that is, in the hope of attracting a buyer.

The cozy bungalow has always been a favorite, but since World War I other, more modern styles have become popular – the quaint Cape Cod or Cotswold cottage, the sprawling ranch house, the slightly larger split-level, and a variety of eclectic suburban homes. The American Dream promises a house for everyone who can afford it.

Owning your own home is not for everyone. Some people prefer the affordability and convenience of apartment living. Here is an arrangement where you can pay your landlord by the month and let him worry about upkeep on the property!

Apartments are usually in good locations and have easy access to parking. In large cities high-rise units are close to places of work, restaurants, and shopping areas. Suburban garden apartments are located away from the center of town and have two or three stories arranged around a landscaped central courtyard. Just like houses, apartments come in sizes, types, and styles to fit every preference.

KANSAS CITY PORCH
KANSAS CITY, MISSOURI
1916

These apartments, nicknamed "Kansas City Porch" because of the triple porticos on either side of the facade, were built along many fashionable boulevards in Kansas City, Missouri, just after 1900. Their spacious floor plans and attractive classical exteriors account for their popularity.

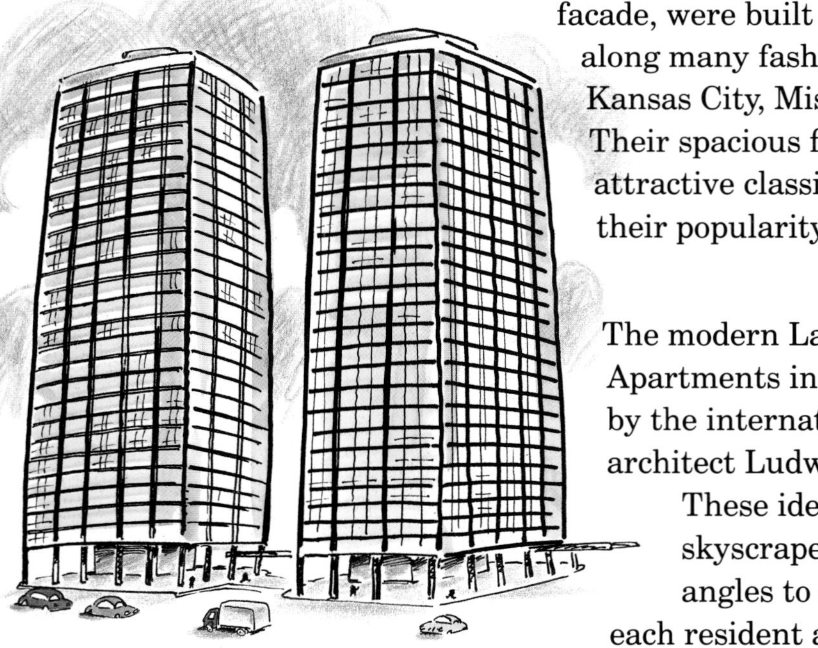

LAKE SHORE DRIVE APARTMENTS
CHICAGO, ILLINOIS
1949-51

The modern Lake Shore Drive Apartments in Chicago were designed by the internationally famous architect Ludwig Mies van der Rohe. These identical glass and metal skyscrapers are set at right angles to one another to allow each resident a view of Lake Michigan and privacy, despite the close quarters.

Loft living has become an ideal housing alternative since the 1960s. At first artists, dancers, and actors sought out these large, vacant floor spaces in downtown warehouses because they offered the extra room they needed for their work. They soon realized that they could save money on rent by living and working in the same place. In the past few years loft living has attracted others who choose to stay in the city rather than flee to the suburbs. The high ceiling, oversized windows, hardwood floors, and open floor plan of the loft make a spacious apartment with great possibilities for creativity.

LOFTS HAVE PLENTY OF 'WIDE OPEN' SPACE.

In Kansas City the Atrium on the Plaza condominiums, designed by Israeli architect Moshe Safdie, offer another solution to apartment living in the city. Reminiscent of the cliff dwellings at Mesa Verde, these modular units are stacked one on top of the other to create a large residential complex. The modules, prefabricated in a factory and assembled on site, are inexpensive and efficient. Sun shades add splashes of color to the otherwise stark concrete, glass, and steel construction.

ATRIUM ON THE PLAZA
KANSAS CITY, MISSOURI
1980

ROW HOUSES

The row house is a compromise between living in a single-family home and living in an apartment. Almost always found in large cities with limited building space, row houses are situated on narrow lots, they share a common or party wall with neighboring houses, and they are two to five stories in height. Available for rent or for purchase, row houses provide small-scale urban living for many people.

"BROWNSTONES"

Brownstones are a kind of row house. They can be found all over New York City. The exteriors vary in design, but the interiors follow basically the same plan: the kitchen is on the basement level, rooms for entertaining are on the second floor, and the private rooms are on the third floor and above. Once they provided housing for middle-income families, but now the New York Brownstones are among the most sophisticated and expensive places to live.

COLUMBIA HEIGHTS
BROOKLYN, NEW YORK
1852

The great Chicago fire of 1871 prompted a building boom in the Hyde Park-Kenwood area south of the city. Most of these row houses had tall basements to keep the living areas above the mud and water of city streets. The builder often varied the facade of each row house with brick or stone patterns or decorated bay windows.

HYDE PARK-KENWOOD HISTORIC DISTRICT
CHICAGO, ILLINOIS
1888

Unique to Pasadena, California, are bungalow courts, a small group of cottages arranged in a U or an L shape around a central courtyard. These single-family residences, developed between 1910 and 1930, were designed in a variety of styles including Craftsman, Mission, Spanish Colonial Revival, Tudor, and Colonial. Like apartments, the courts provided security and a sense of community within their own small neighborhood setting.

GARTZ COURT
PASADENA, CALIFORNIA
1910

PREFAB HOUSES

Innovator R. Buckminster Fuller devoted the greater part of his life to creating the ideal house for an industrialized society. He sought a structure that would be completely prefabricated in a factory and, once assembled, could have a controlled environment suitable for any temperature or place.

Fuller realized this dream in the Dymaxion House, whose name is a combination of "dynamic" and "maximum." The prototype, built for him by Beech Aircraft Company in Wichita, Kansas, in 1944, was adapted from a 1927 design. It could be erected anywhere because it needed no foundation. No one part weighed more than ten pounds, and any piece could be installed by a single worker. All utility rooms were prefabricated so they could be hung on the structural frame. A one-piece molded bathroom, completely mechanical kitchen and laundry, and rotating shelving system were among the house's unusual features. Completely self-sufficient, the house did not need city water, electrical, or sewage systems and had its own ventilating system. The Dymaxion house could be taken apart and mailed in a tube. At a cost of $6,500 to build, this was an economical, labor-saving, and environmentally conscious habitat.

DYMAXION II
BEECH AIRCRAFT CORP.
WICHITA, KANSAS
1944

An alternative design still used today is Fuller's Geodesic Dome. The prefabricated structure is basically a geometric stick frame made of plastic or metal connectors and filler panels made of lightweight aluminum, Plexiglas, wood – or just about anything! Sometimes a "skin" of vinyl or cloth tarpaulin is stretched over the frame. Mail-order kits are available from construction companies and can be assembled by a few workers in less than two days. The Geodesic Dome can be any size from quite small to as large as the United States Pavilion at the 1967 Montreal World's Fair. Light in weight, yet sturdy and easy to construct, Fuller's designs are a creative and economical housing solution.

Can you imagine a house with wheels? What about a house that's made in a factory and sold in a showroom like a brand new car? If you're in the market for a house that's ready to move when you are, the mobile home is for you!

The small travel trailer, first introduced in the late 1920s and early 1930s as the perfect vacation companion, hitched to the back of a car or truck and offered a place to cook and sleep. Soon the larger recreational vehicle (RV) was developed for cross-country travel. It comes complete with its own kitchenette, bathroom, bedroom, and built-in engine. A great way to see the United States from your living room, but a real gas guzzler!

A good idea is a good idea, however, and for many people the rolling vacation home has become the perfect permanent home. Its low cost, easy maintenance, and suitability for any location make it a popular housing alternative. Completely prefabricated, the mobile home or "manufactured house" is precut and partially assembled, then transported by special truck to the building site. The mobile home is pretty narrow because it cannot be wider than the width of the highway over which it travels. Sometimes mobile home units are put together on location to make a more spacious house. Once the house is completely assembled, it is hooked up to electrical, water, and disposal systems. Most mobile homeowners live in trailer courts, a neighborhood of mobile homes that provides the necessary utilities.

Just like any house, the mobile home reflects the owner's taste because it can be decorated with awnings, shutters, colors, and gardens. Often the mobile home is made larger and more permanent by room or porch additions or even a gable roof. Today several million Americans live in mobile homes. In fact, manufactured housing accounts for one-quarter of all single-family housing produced each year. Uniquely American, the mobile home is an affordable and adaptable place to hang your hat.

How do you heat your house? Your stove? The water for your bath? You probably use oil, gas, or electricity. When these energy sources are high priced or in short supply, people think about building a house that uses natural resources that are readily available and less costly.

Solar heating, heat provided by the sun, is one popular and practical alternative. Solar systems are active or passive.

The active solar system uses mechanical equipment to convert heat, store it, and then distribute it. The sun's warmth is absorbed through glass boxes or "solar panels" on the south-facing part of the roof or house. The heat is absorbed either by water that is transferred through pipes to a hot water tank or by air that is pumped to a rock-filled basement storage area that acts as a furnace. From there the hot air is released through vents all over the house as needed.

Passive systems are less costly than active solar systems because no special equipment is needed to distribute the heat. Large areas of glass in the south wall absorb heat and distribute it throughout living spaces to warm the house. Extra heat is stored in "thermal masses" such as thick cement floors, walls, or even large containers of water to release warmth at night or on cold days.

Both active and passive solar houses are shielded from summer sun by broad roof overhangs, glazed windows, or blinds. Warm air is ventilated through skylights or sliding glass doors. Floor plans are usually more open so that warm and cool air can circulate more freely throughout the house.

Many older homes have been adapted for solar energy by adding a sun room or a greenhouse. Such a room can collect heat for cold evenings and can be shut off during the day to keep the house from getting too warm. Only part of the home benefits from passive solar energy, but heating costs are still reduced.

The energy crisis encouraged architects to reconsider another type of housing that takes advantage of both solar heating and natural insulation: the earth-sheltered house. Like the pioneer dugout, the house is surrounded by the earth as much as possible to provide a constant, comfortable temperature.

EARTH SHELTERED HOUSE

FANTASY HOUSES

How would you like to live in a house that looks like a shoe? Or an elephant? What about a house made out of trash? It's possible even though it seems impossible. Designers can create their wildest, most original, most unconventional fantasies by breaking with tradition. Some start with an idea or a shape in mind and build from the outside in. But sometimes the shape develops room by room without much thought to the appearance of the exterior. These buildings are built from the inside out, and they look added-on-to. Whatever form they take, these houses add fun and variety to our urban landscape.

Built as a tourist attraction in 1881, Lucy the Elephant is still standing 100 years later. As tall as a six-story building, her wooden frame is covered with nearly 12,000 square feet of tin. A domed room filling her belly is illuminated by a huge skylight overhead. Spiral staircases wind up her hind legs, and giant portholes fill her eyes. Another stairway goes up to the howdah or basket for passengers on Lucy's back, which serves as an observation deck.

LUCY THE ELEPHANT
MARGATE, NEW JERSEY
1881

Architect Michael Reynolds uses his imagination to build Earthship houses that are dug out of the hillside. The whole southern wall of each house is enclosed with double-pane glass. Trapped sunlight warms all the rooms. Special cells on the roof collect and convert sunshine into enough electrical energy to operate all the household appliances. Each home is insulated by three-foot-thick walls made of old beer cans and tires filled with dirt. The demand for these earthships is so great that Reynolds is now selling plans for a do-it-yourself model.

EARTHSHIP
TAOS, NEW MEXICO

Colonel Mahlon Haines built the Shoe House in 1949 as a home and as a novel advertisement for his shoe business. More than 40 feet long and covered with cement stucco, the Shoe House has a rooftop terrace overlooking the surrounding countryside; windows are made of stained glass featuring shoe designs. Even the mailbox and the doghouse are shaped like shoes!

THE SHOE HOUSE
HALAM, PENNSYLVANIA
1949

Architect Bruce Goff designed the Nicol House in Kansas City, Missouri, to look like a modern tepee. The floor plan of the house is octagonal. The rooms on the main floor center on a sunken fireplace, a fountain, and a pool. Wall-to-wall carpeting on the floor and on the steps provides comfortable seating. Windows are placed high on the wall for privacy. Skylights provide additional light.

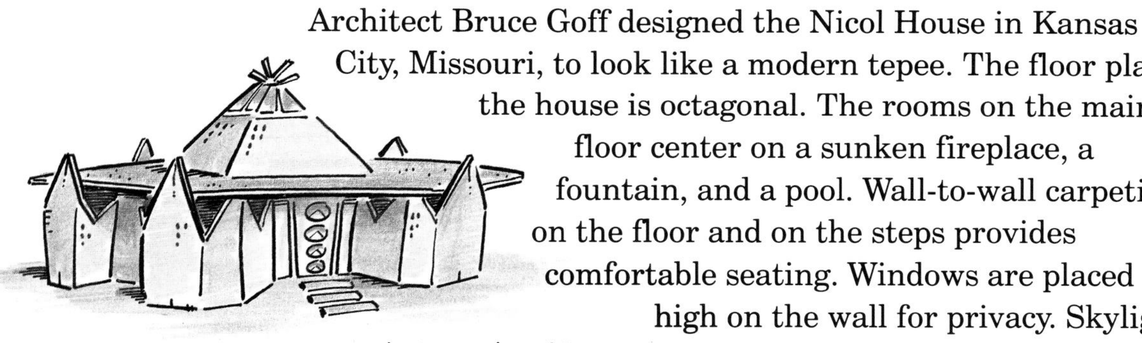

THE NICOL HOUSE
KANSAS CITY, MISSOURI
1967

Constant breezes, splendid views of the horizon, no street traffic noise, freedom from mowing the lawn and shoveling snow... Where is this paradise? In a houseboat! Complete with kitchen, living room, bedroom, bath, and perhaps a rooftop garden, the houseboat has been a popular residential alternative since before the turn of the century.

WELCOME

HOUSEBOATS FLOATING
ALONG THE FLORIDA COAST

CITY OF THE

Some designers are thinking about the future. In Arizona, architect Paolo Soleri is creating an entire city, Arcosanti, where people live and work. The village depends on "arcology," the idea that architecture and economy will work together to build a better living environment. Soleri directs the plan of all buildings, constructing innovative and climate-conscious structures decorated with colorful patterns. Arcosanti is different from most cities, which develop over a long period of time and where houses, churches, and commercial buildings are designed by many different people.

Artists, students, and scholars visit Arcosanti to attend special seminars and workshops conducted by staff members under the direction of Soleri. Beautiful bells and sculpture are made for sale at Arcosanti and elsewhere to help pay for the continued growth of this experimental community. The many people who live and work at Arcosanti will benefit from the greenhouses that provide food and help in energy conservation and production. The buildings of Arcosanti are compact and situated close together, leaving the surrounding landscape free for agriculture and recreation.

If Soleri's vision is ever fully realized, Arcosanti will be an example of an economical, environmentally conscious community that can offer a rich living experience for its residents and some lessons for all of us about the development of our present and future communities.

HOUSES FOR THE HOMELESS

We have considered many different types of houses from all over the United States in this book. Although they may not look alike, they all have a roof and doors and they provide a place to sleep. Many people in America have no home at all. Their bed is on the street, in a doorway, under a plastic sheet, or maybe inside a cardboard box. Some spend the night on a park bench, in a subway or train station, or on a cot in a crowded city mission or Salvation Army center. If the weather is poor, these people get wet or cold or suffer from the heat. Thousands, possibly millions, of homeless people are out there right now in your city and in other cities across our country.

PORTABLE SLEEPER

Something is being done to help these people. Our government and concerned citizens are developing many new projects to fight against homelessness. Here are some examples of what they have accomplished (or tried to accomplish) so far.

Warm and safe, this sleeping space designed by Bob McNamara and Joe Beckett has its own pillow and a two-inch-thick foam mattress. Weighing only four pounds, it folds up completely and can be easily carried when not in use.

Architect Christopher Rose has designed single-family cottages for Charleston, South Carolina. These prefabricated units can be either lined up side by side or stacked up on top of each other. They are a good example of quality, low-cost living space. The Work Program, a not-for-profit organization in Charleston, is finding a way to build even more of these houses. Homeless people will be hired for construction jobs and receive job skill training so that they will ultimately be able to afford a home like this for themselves.

FAMILY COTTAGE IN CHARLESTON

People helping people is what Habitat for Humanity is all about. In this innovative program, volunteers build houses in more than 900 cities in 38 different countries. The families who live in the new homes pay back the full cost of their houses over time without paying any interest to Habitat. The monthly payments are determined by the cost of the house. President and Mrs. Jimmy Carter have been strong supporters of Habitat for many years. Through their efforts they have encouraged others to work on its behalf. Habitat for Humanity celebrated its 15th Anniversary in 1991; completed its 15,000th home on June 20, 1992; and looks forward to finishing construction on its 20,000th home in April of 1993.

Concerned about two homeless men camping in the parking lot outside his office, California architect Donald MacDonald designed the City Sleeper. This 4-foot-wide, 4-foot-high, and 8-foot-long weatherproof plywood shelter comes equipped with windows, closet, shelf, and foam mattress. The side entry panel can be raised to provide a canopy for shade. At a cost of $500, the "City Sleeper" provides privacy, comfort, and a safe place out of the rain.

MacDonald has also introduced another idea for affordable single-family housing: the Starter Home. This small residence has one room and a loft, measures 300 square feet, and costs about $12,000 without the land. The unit has a compact kitchen and bathroom and a fireplace capable of heating the entire space. Skylights and glass doors give a feeling of openness. The Starter Home is easily put together and can be expanded to accommodate more units for more space. MacDonald considers these homes a real housing alternative for homeless people, college students, the elderly, or first-time house buyers.

PART TWO

When we talk about the style of a house, we are describing the way the house looks. When all the architectural elements – floor plan, roof, window shapes, brick patterns – work together to create a particular look, it can be characterized as a style. Different styles have been introduced at different times and places throughout history. These styles often overlap one another, and some are so popular that they continue to be built year after year.

GEORGIAN STYLE

DRAYTON HALL
CHARLESTON, SOUTH CAROLINA
1738

Although the very best example of a style is usually designed and introduced by an architect, variations on that design will certainly crop up in neighborhoods from coast to coast. Consider, for example, the Prairie Style houses of Frank Lloyd Wright, which have been adapted for varying materials, locations, and budgets by other architects and contractors across America.

PRAIRIE STYLE

FRANK LLOYD WRIGHT
HOME and STUDIO
OAK PARK, ILLINOIS
1889

Sometimes the need for a certain type of structure determines how a house looks. The house barn or log cabin is a good example of this. Then, too, the look of a house might depend on available building materials, social customs, or traditions brought to this country by our immigrant ancestors. These styles might only be found in a certain part of the country and built by a particular group of people. Houses that fall within this category are referred to as vernacular.

HORACE BAKER HOUSE
OREGON CITY, OREGON
1856

Many American house styles are described and illustrated on the following pages. While you read and look at the pictures, try to remember what makes each house unique. We will use that information later when we try to determine what styles are in your own hometown.

COLONIAL STYLES, 1600–1820

NEW ENGLAND COLONIAL, 1600–1700

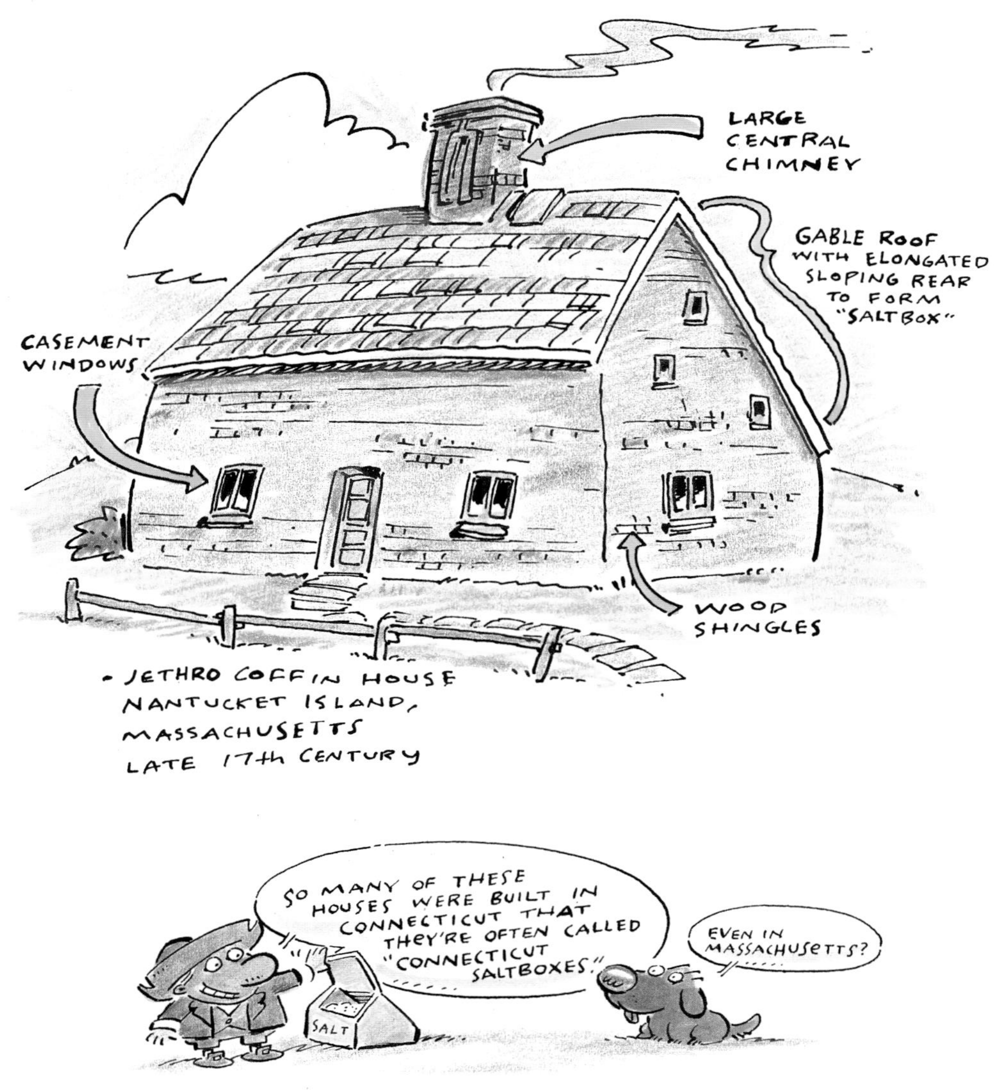

The need for protection against the cold New England winters dictated the design of the 17th-century Colonial house – small rooms arranged around a large central chimney, small casement windows, and low ceilings. A room across the rear of the house, called a lean-to, was often added to extend living space. Over time this room became a part of the house design. In larger houses of this type, the upper floor extends over the lower floors, creating an overhang or jetty. Windows in the gable end provide light for this upstairs area. The outside walls are covered with unpainted clapboard or hand-split shingles, as is the roof.

SOUTHERN COLONIAL, 1600–1700

The brick or wood-frame Southern Colonial house is usually one room deep and crowned with a high gable roof. Borrowings from medieval architecture can be seen in the curved or stepped gable ends, multiple chimney stacks on either side of the house, and different brick patterns used in combination for a decorative effect. Classical details such as arches over windows and doorways are common, too.

—BACON'S CASTLE
SURRY COUNTY
VIRGINIA
1665

SPANISH COLONIAL AND MONTERREY STYLE, 1600–1840

Typically one story in height, the Spanish Colonial house has thick walls made of adobe brick or of stone covered with stucco. Windows are small and sparse, but exterior doorways are plentiful. A long covered porch runs across the front of the house and is accented by square, rough-cut porch posts with brackets. Roof types vary; the most common is a low gable covered with red Spanish tiles or, like the Palace of the Governors, a flat roof with parapet wall. Notice the wooden roof beams or vigas projecting through the parapet wall.

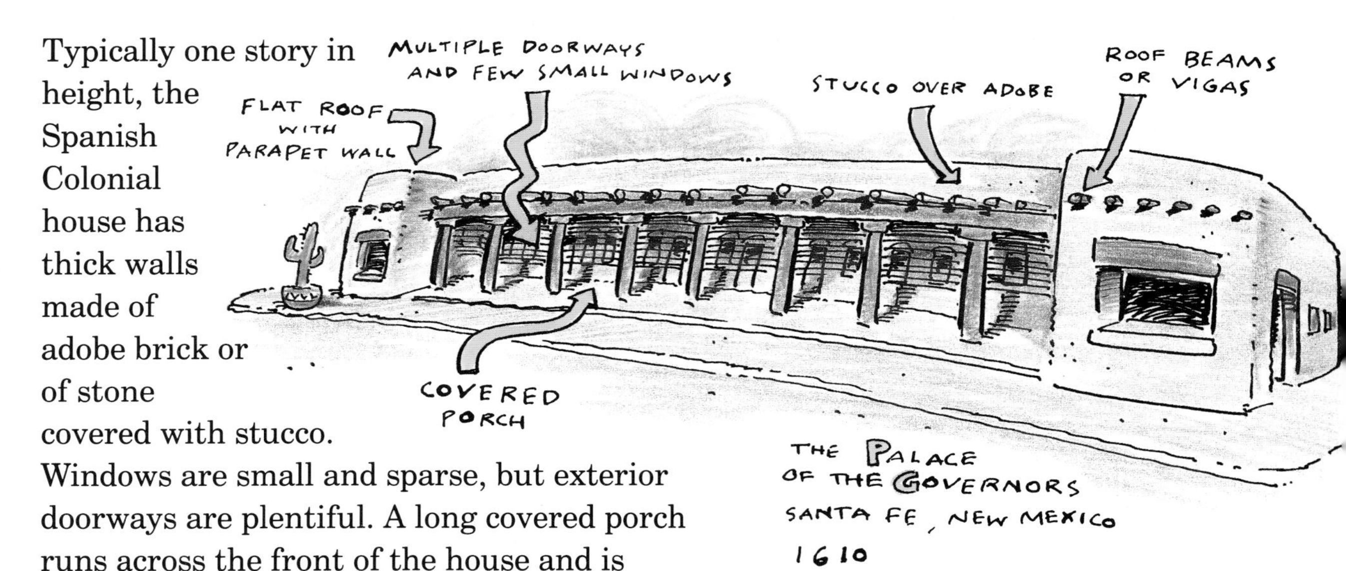

The 19th-century Monterey Style is a variation of this design. The two-story house is covered with shingles and has a broad hip roof and exterior porches across the front of the first and perhaps the second floor. An enclosed garden or patio is often located at the rear of the house. The Monterey Style took its name from the city in California where so many of these houses were built.

FRENCH COLONIAL, 1700–1830

French Colonial houses are characterized by vertical log construction. The logs, planed on all four sides, are set upright into a foundation. The spaces between the logs are filled with a mixture of rocks and mortar. A gallery or shaded porch around the house provides cool outdoor living space. The houses have casement windows and, typically, a pair of French entry doors. The Saucier house has a pavilion roof, which is like two hipped roofs, one on top of the other.

The French plantation house, a variation of this type, has similar characteristics, but the basement floor is above ground. The gallery is still a major part of the house design, as is the exterior stairway leading up to the main entrance.

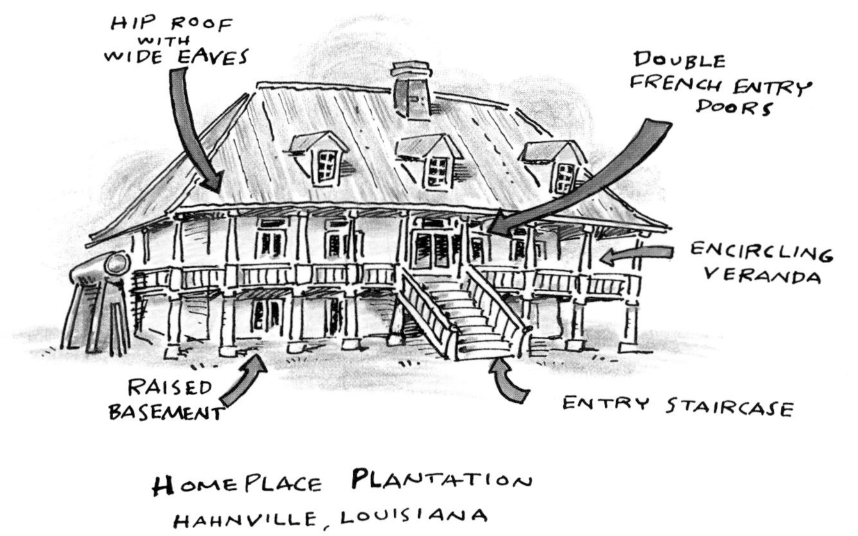

DUTCH COLONIAL, 1700–1830

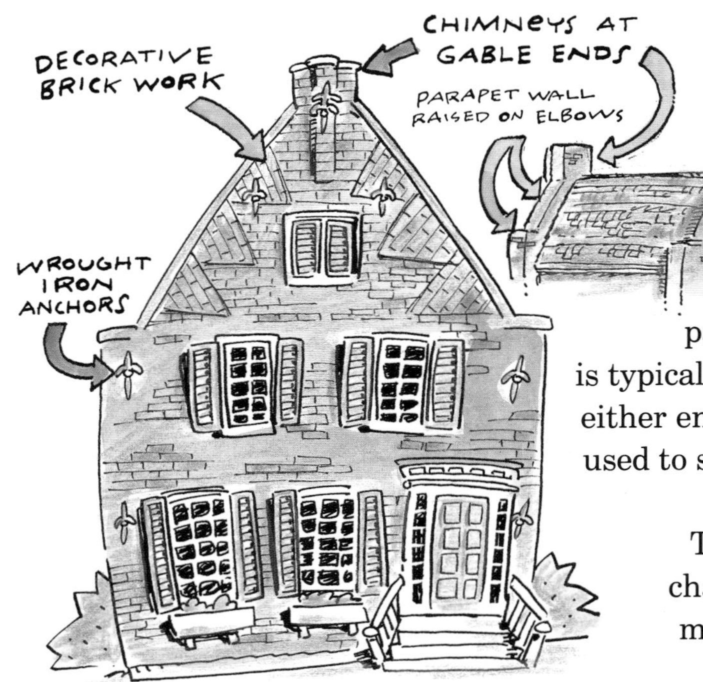

ABRAHAM YATES HOUSE
SCHENECTADY, NEW YORK

Eighteenth-century Dutch Colonial architecture falls into two style categories. The first, seen in the Abraham Yates House, features brick with steep, straight-edge gables that face sideways. A parapet wall raised on elbows at the corners is typical of this style, as is the pair of chimneys at either end of the roof. Wrought iron anchors are used to secure the bricks.

The second and more familiar style, characteristic of the late 18th century, was more spacious and better suited to country living. Here the exterior walls are of stone or wooden weatherboard, and the gambrel roof has a wide overhang. A front porch is shaded by the slope of the eaves. This style remained popular among homeowners well into the 20th century.

LEFFERTS HOMESTEAD
BROOKLYN N.Y.
1783

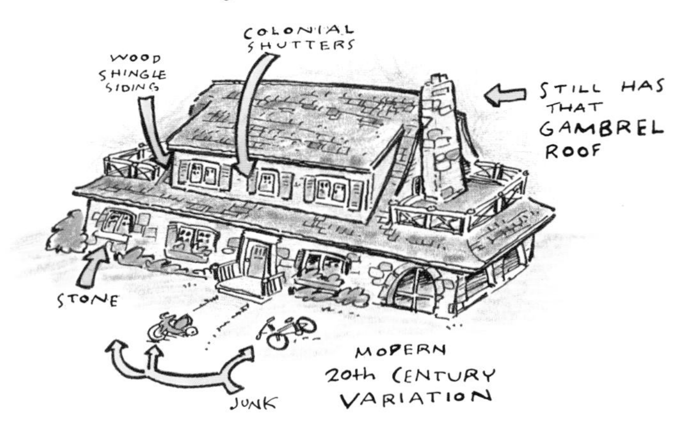

MODERN 20th CENTURY VARIATION

GEORGIAN, 1700–1800

The Georgian Style, which dominated the East Coast in the 18th century, is identified by its square shape and symmetrical arrangement of doors and windows. Constructed of brick, smooth stone, and sometimes clapboard, Georgian houses are usually two stories high and covered by a gable, hip, or gambrel roof. There is often an elaborate entryway and paneled doorway, sometimes with a glass transom or sidelights. Often the entire central section is highlighted by a projecting portico supported by colossal columns or pilasters. A Palladian or Venetian window frequently provides a dramatic focus. Sash windows have as few as nine and as many as 20 panes of glass each. The style features rich classical detailing around all openings, under the cornice, on the edges of the building, and often on the roof.

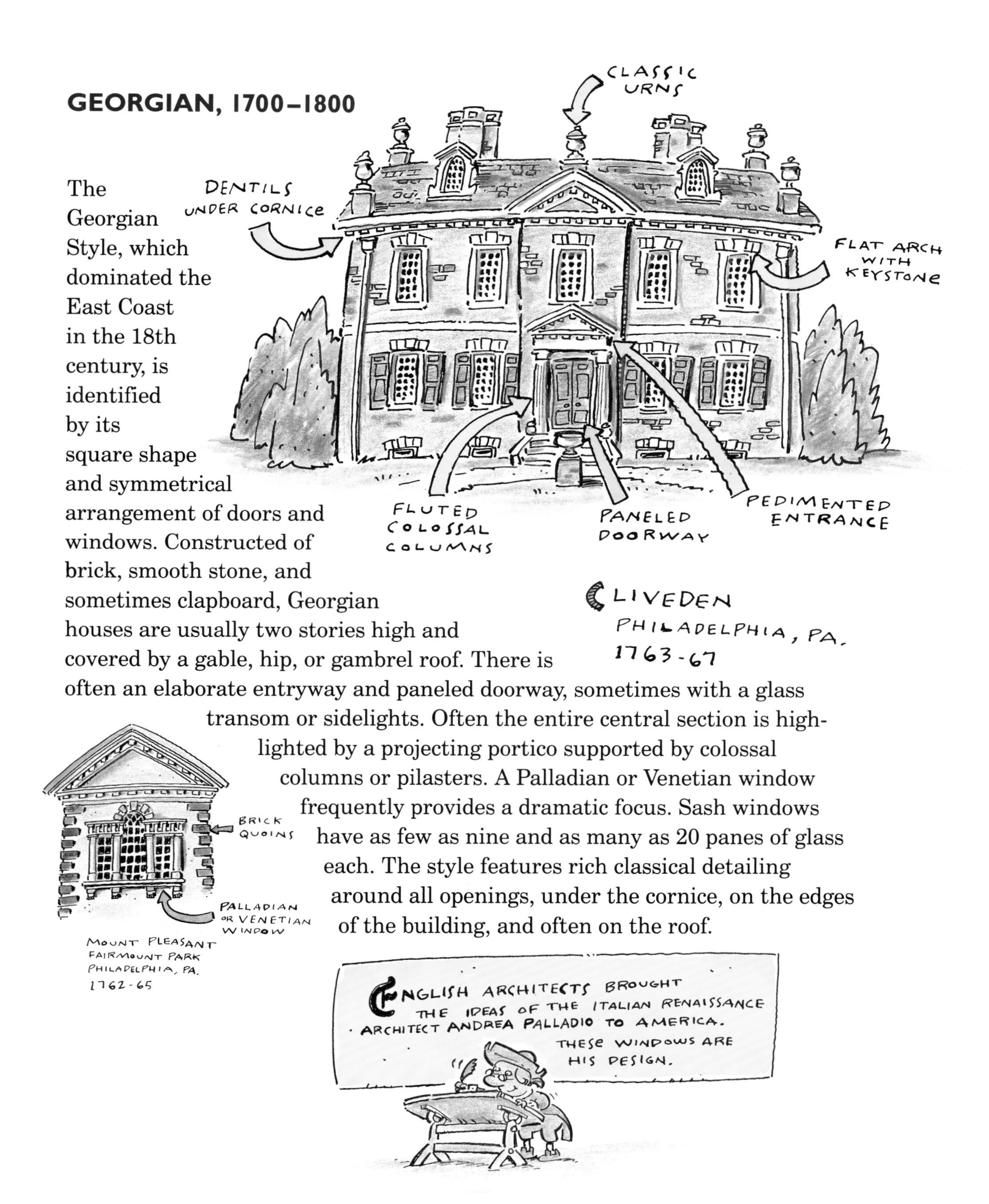

FEDERAL OR ADAM STYLE, 1780–1820

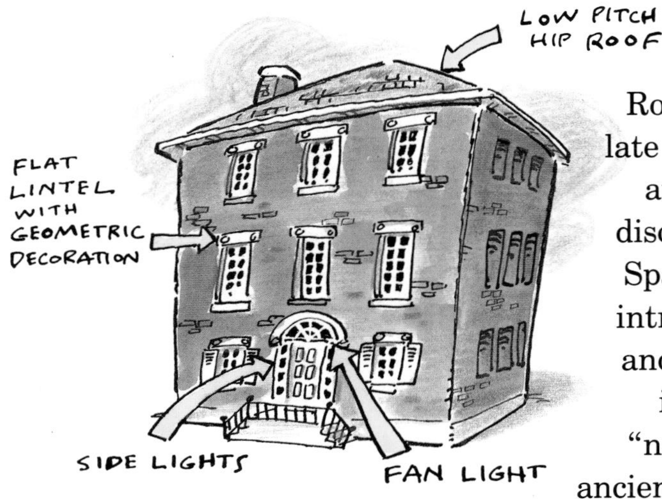

The Federal Style is derived from the delicate interior decorations of Robert and James Adam in Britain in the late 18th century. The startling excavations at Herculaneum and Pompeii and the discovery of the Palace of Diocletian at Spalato near the turn of the century introduced new ideas about ancient design and architecture that the Adams brothers incorporated into their work. This "neoclassical," or new way of looking at ancient art forms, became known in America as the Federal Style.

Federal houses are two to three stories high, are rectangular in shape, and have projecting wings. A shallow hip roof is common, and the roof may have a balustrade. Decoration, both inside and out, is lighter and more delicate than that of the Georgian Style. It may comprise swags, urns, wheat, garlands, and geometric patterns. Doorways are framed with fan lights and sidelights, while large bay windows may accent the facade. Inside rooms are oval, circular, rectangular, or polygonal in shape.

JEFFERSONIAN CLASSICISM (OR ROMAN REVIVAL), 1790–1830

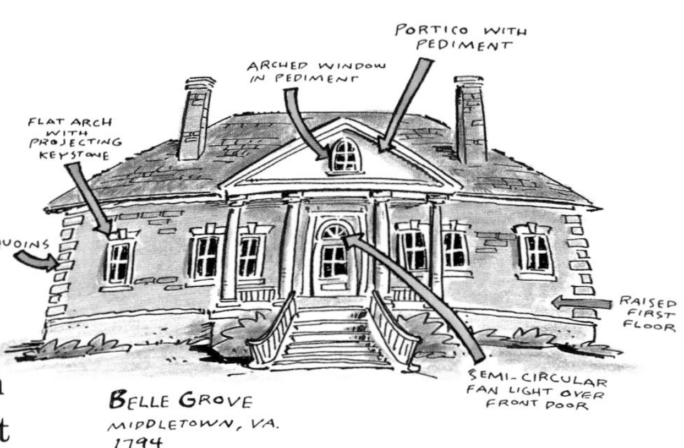

Jeffersonian Classicism was shaped by Thomas Jefferson and named after him, but it took its inspiration from the architecture of republican Rome. Jefferson's idea was to link our new buildings as well as our form of government with this ancient civilization. Homes and public buildings were designed in this style based on Roman temples and on the work of the Italian Renaissance architect Andrea Palladio.

Common features of this style include a raised first floor, like the podium of a temple, and a portico with four columns supporting a large pediment. An arched window or fan light often appears in the center of the pediment and sometimes over the front door as well. Ornamentation is minimal; moldings are painted white for contrast against the exterior, which is typically red brick.

Monticello, Jefferson's house, is one of the most beautiful examples of this style. Jefferson greatly admired Palladio's Villa Rotunda, built in 1567–70, and Monticello shows its influence. The house has two raised porticos, a central dome, and wings on each side. The plan of the interior, with its many polygonal rooms, is reflected in the angular shape of the exterior. Classical details are seen in the arched and circular windows, the Doric porch columns, and the detailed entablature above the columns.

REVIVAL STYLES AND ROMANTIC IDEAS, 1820–1920

GREEK REVIVAL, 1820–80

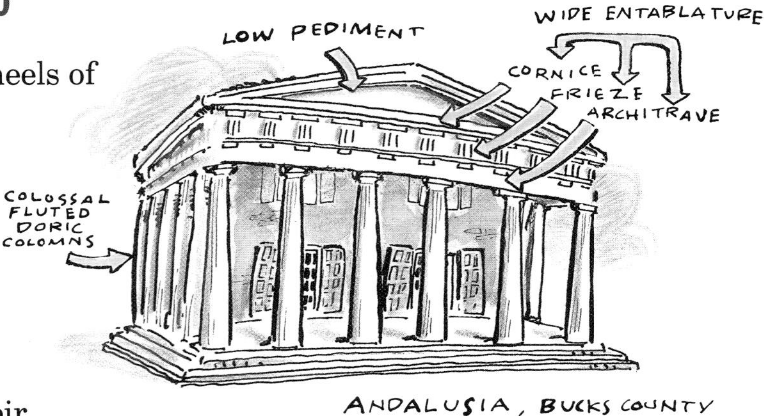

Greek Revival followed on the heels of Jeffersonian Classicism, and its appeal was immediate and widespread. Here was a building style whose clean, strong lines and simple, solid shapes were the foundation on which Americans, like the ancient Greeks, would build their democracy. It was accessible to everyone. Buildings that followed the style in its purest form mimicked the temples of ancient Greece. The first Greek Revival building in America was the Bank of Pennsylvania, built by Benjamin Henry Latrobe in Philadelphia in 1798.

The Greek Revival style had many variations, but common to almost every home regardless of size are classical columns, when possible, and the use of white paint to simulate marble. The design of Andalusia, a beautiful High-Style example, is based on an ancient Greek temple. In this house, fluted colossal Doric columns support the wide entablature and low pediment. Perhaps the most frequently used design element is the pedimented or flat-roofed portico supported by two to four columns. Doorways often have sidelights and may be crowned by a rectangular transom. Arches are never used; instead, window and doorway surrounds are mostly straight-edged, and ornament is kept to a minimum.

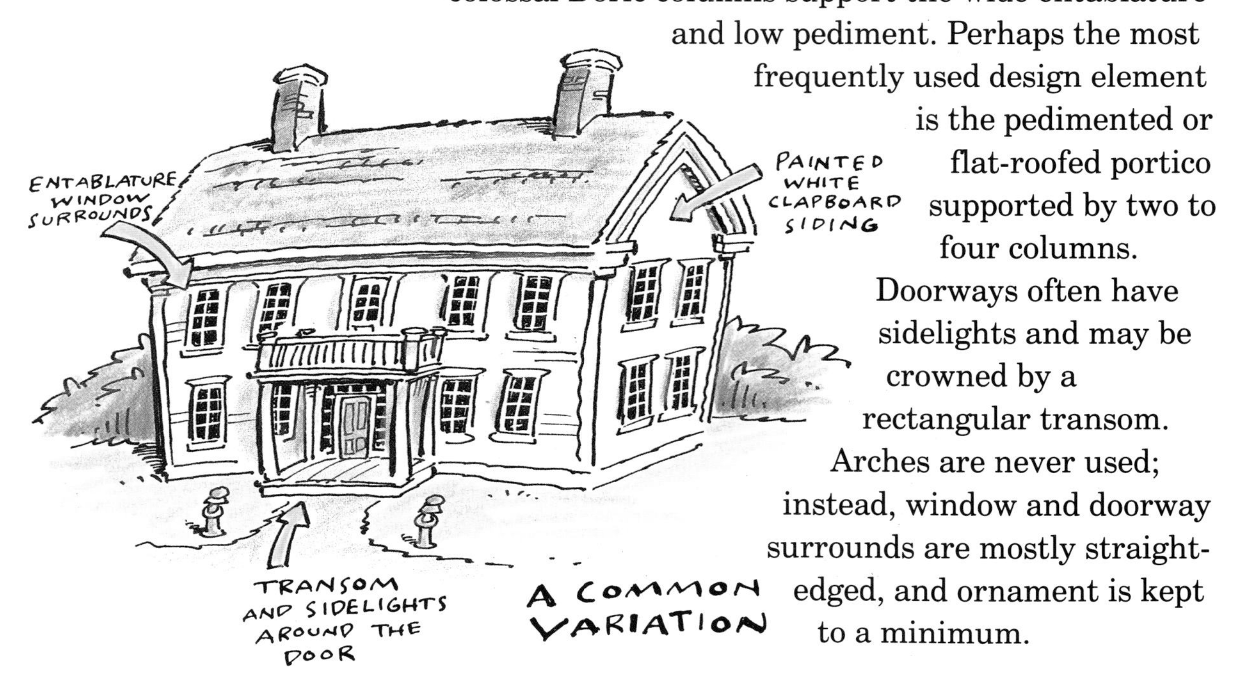

GOTHIC REVIVAL, 1830–60

The Romantic movement in England prompted by the writings of Sir Walter Scott and the fascination with the Middle Ages contributed to a renewed interest in Gothic architecture. Gothic Revival was a fanciful, magical style freed from the absolute correctness of the classical revivals. It was widely used for churches, colleges, and other public buildings, but many homes also were built in the Gothic Style.

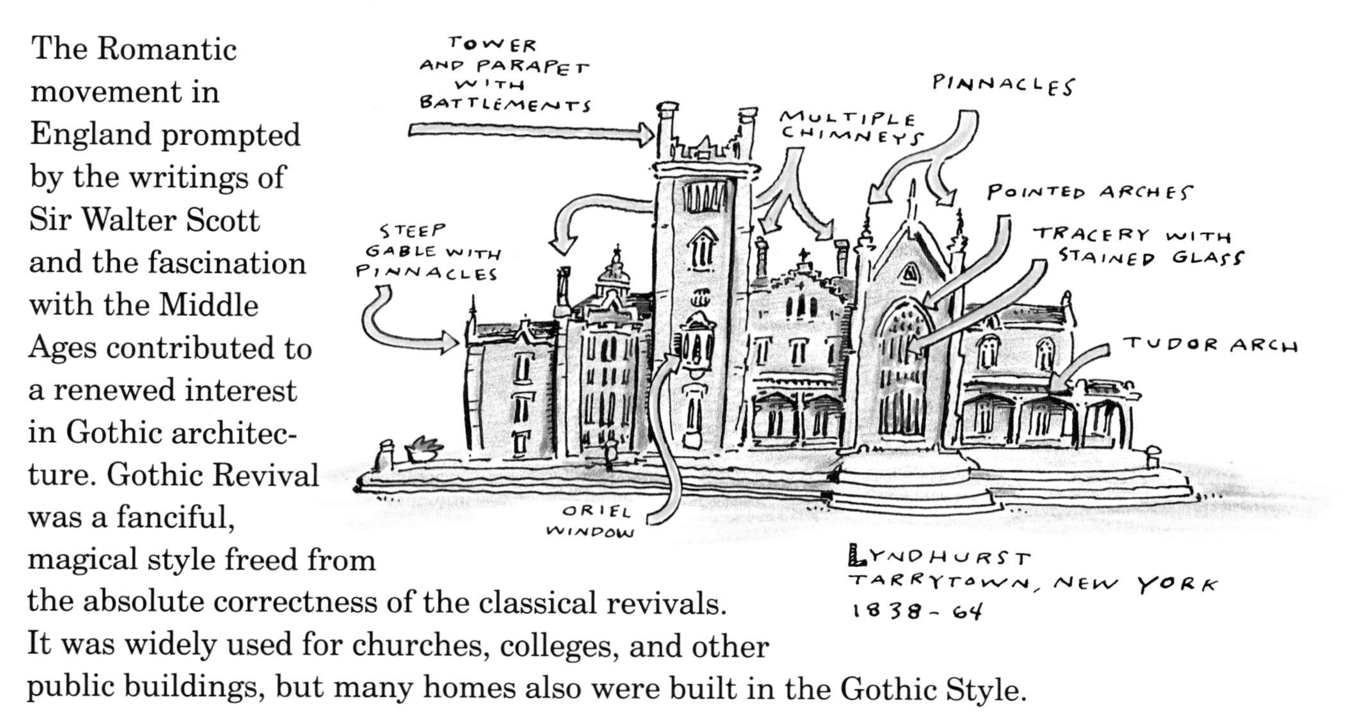

Lyndhurst, designed by Alexander Jackson Davis, is an example of the style at its most majestic. The house has a rambling silhouette highlighted by battlemented towers and parapets, steep gables, clustered chimneys, pinnacles, and verandas. The pointed-arch windows are filled with lacey cut stone tracery and stained glass.

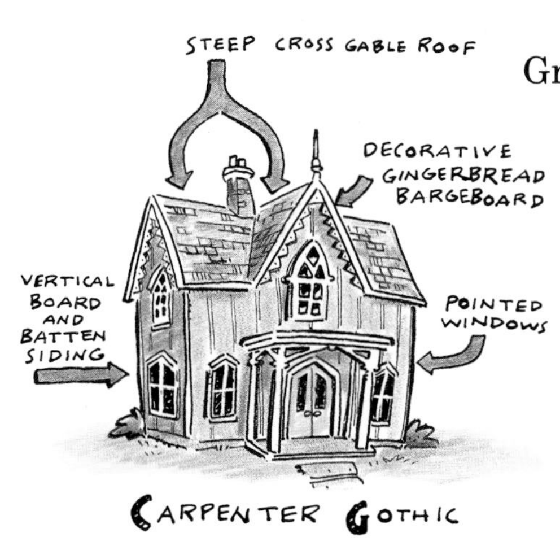

Grand homes like Lyndhurst were rare, however, and many "Carpenter Gothic" cottages were built according to pattern-book models. The newly invented scroll saw allowed carpenters to create the delicate bargeboard trim called "gingerbread," which hangs from the gable end of these houses. Pointed windows with tracery are common, as is vertical board-and-batten siding. Homes are often painted, in pale shades of grey or blue.

ITALIANATE STYLE, 1830–1880

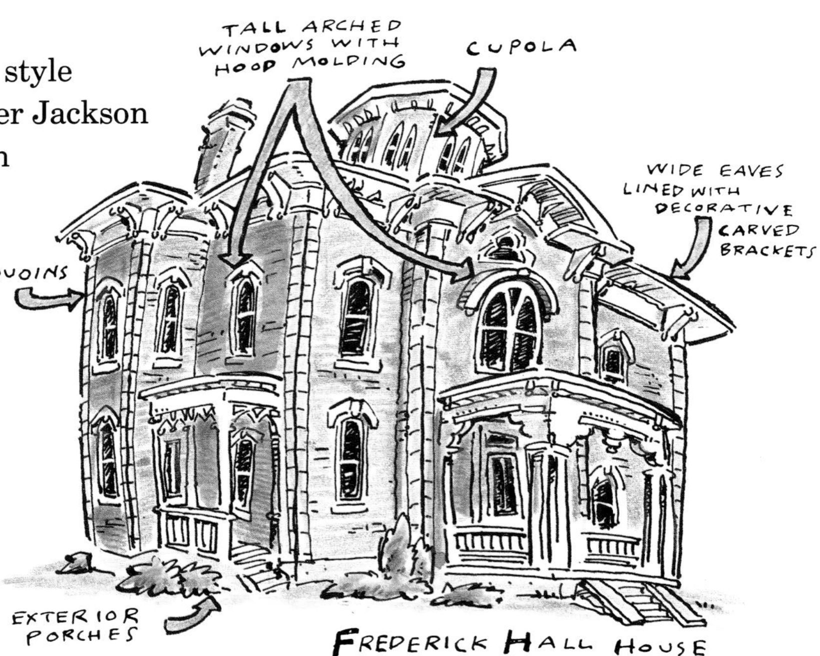

FREDERICK HALL HOUSE
IONIA, MICHIGAN
1870

Another picturesque style designed by Alexander Jackson Davis and featured in the pattern books of Andrew Jackson Downing is the Italianate. Boxy in shape and no less than two to three stories high, these houses have wide eaves lined with decorative carved brackets supporting a shallow hipped roof. They often have a cupola or an entrance tower. Windows on the first floor are framed with ornamental surrounds. Porches and balconies are frequent. Houses in this style were generally built of brick or frame covered with stucco. The style was so popular that it was quickly adapted to houses of all sizes and types and to office buildings. The commercial buildings were often fashioned out of cast iron and can be found in business districts from coast to coast.

A COMMON VARIATION
LATE 19th CENTURY

OCTAGON STYLE, 1850–70

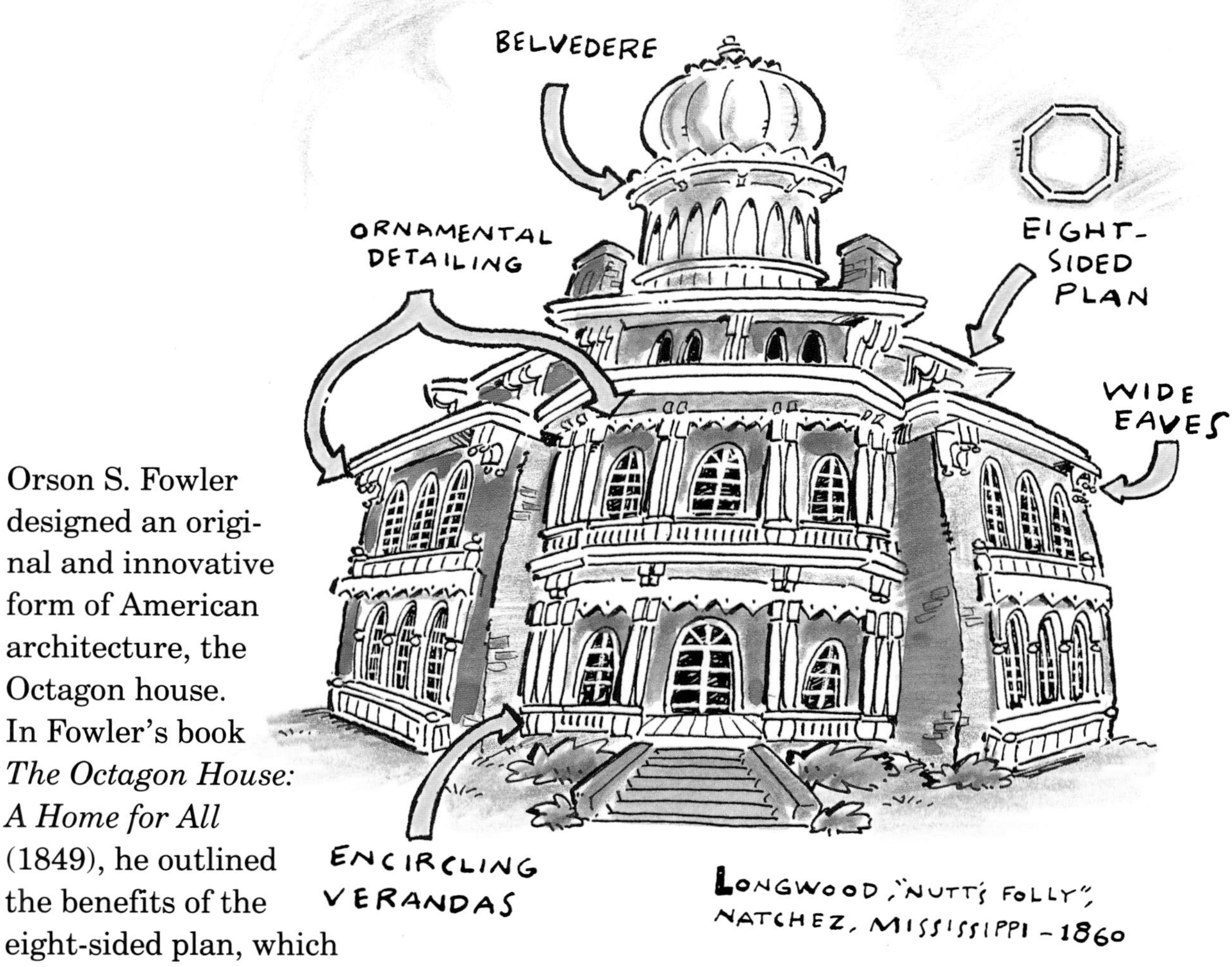

Orson S. Fowler designed an original and innovative form of American architecture, the Octagon house. In Fowler's book *The Octagon House: A Home for All* (1849), he outlined the benefits of the eight-sided plan, which allows for plenty of air circulation and sunlight within the structure and a good view from every room. Interior rooms are square, for the most part, with leftover triangular space tucked into the corners. An interior stairwell ascends from the ground floor to the rooftop belvedere. The two- to three-story house is usually encircled by verandas on each floor, with the wide eaves of the roof or balconies providing shade. Italianate or Greek Revival detailing is common, with decorative brackets, arched windows, and columns adorning the exterior. Although the Octagon never achieved the popularity of other styles of that time, some very beautiful and interesting residences were constructed.

COLONIAL REVIVAL, 1870–1920

The Colonial Revival incorporates all previous styles into one harmonious design. It is often quite difficult to tell the original from the revival except that certain elements may be emphasized or used in new combinations. Oak Alley is a fine though early example of this style. Note in particular the grand two-story colonnade that wraps around the exterior of the house. The influence of the Federal Style can be seen in the double French entry doors on the first and second floors with their semicircular fan lights and engaged pilasters.

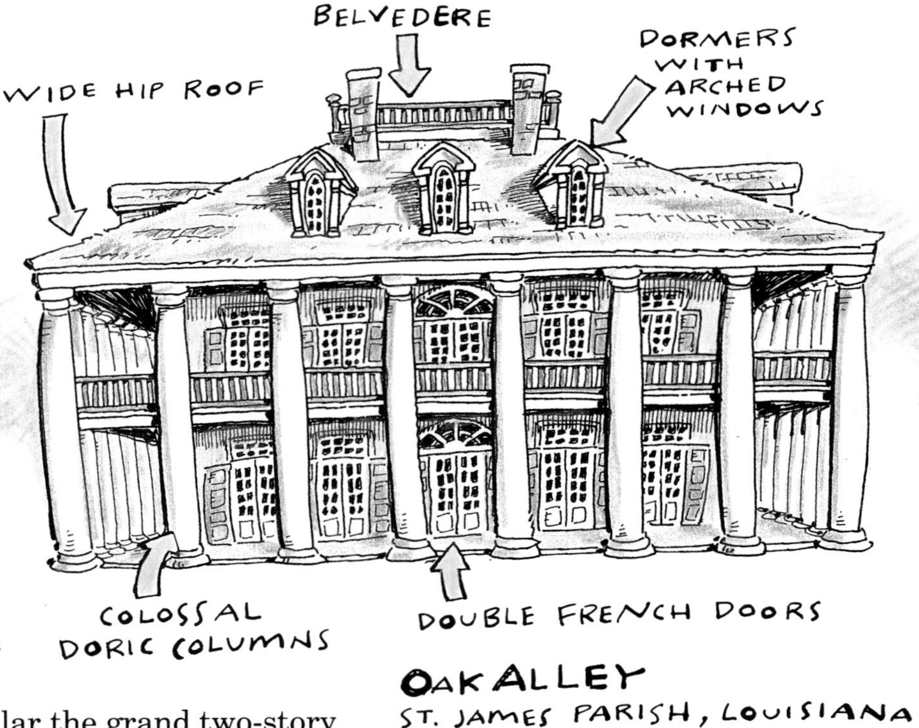

A beautiful urban example of Colonial Revival can be seen in the brick Woodrow Wilson House in Washington, D.C.

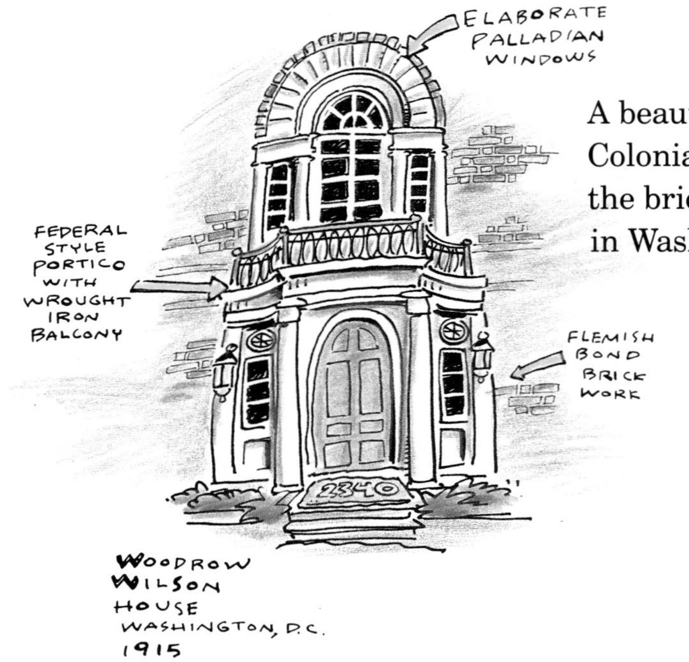

VICTORIAN, 1860–1900

SECOND EMPIRE STYLE, 1860–90

The Second Empire Style was imported from France, where it had been introduced during the regime of Emperor Napoleon III (1852 – 70). The grandiose buildings of this period are characterized by the distinctive mansard roof designed by the 17th–century French architect François Mansart. This roof was tall enough to accommodate an attic story, so it nearly always has dormers to let in light. The roof itself is often covered with patterned tile. The general profile of the structure is dramatic and three dimensional, with emphasis on color, texture, and sculptural detail.

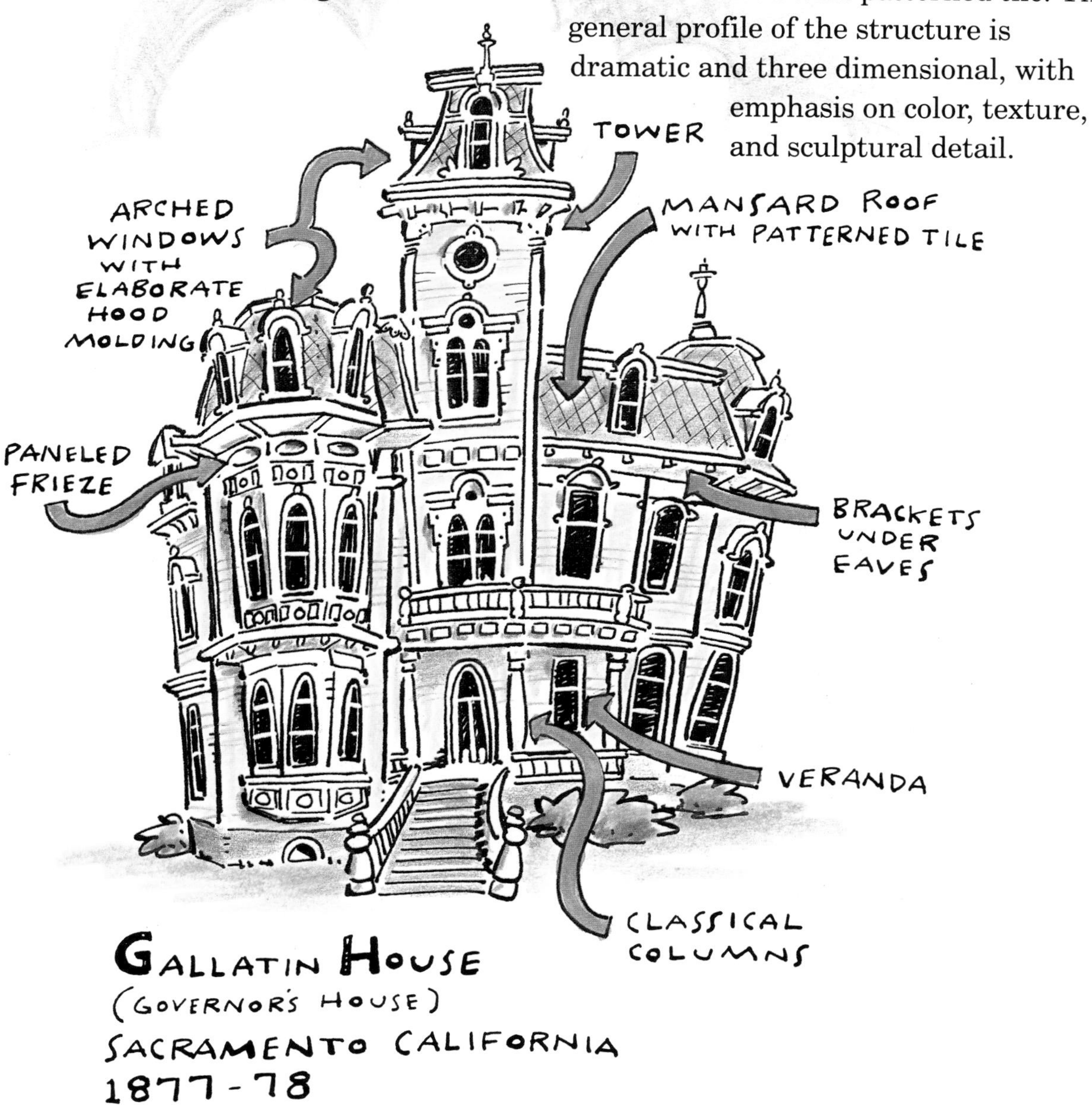

GALLATIN HOUSE
(GOVERNOR'S HOUSE)
SACRAMENTO CALIFORNIA
1877-78

EASTERN STICK STYLE, 1860–90

Constructed entirely of wood, the Stick Style house is characterized by horizontal, vertical, and diagonal boards, or sticks, that crisscross the exterior. These pieces of wood look like the skeleton, or outside structural supports of the house, but they are mostly decorative except for the wooden posts and braces beneath the front porch roof. Surface decoration is enhanced by clapboard on the exterior wall surfaces. Roofs are steeply pitched gables or cross gables, often with towers or large dormers jutting above the roof line. The overhanging eaves are braced with purlins. The silhouette of the house is asymmetrical and picturesque, full of interesting shapes and angles.

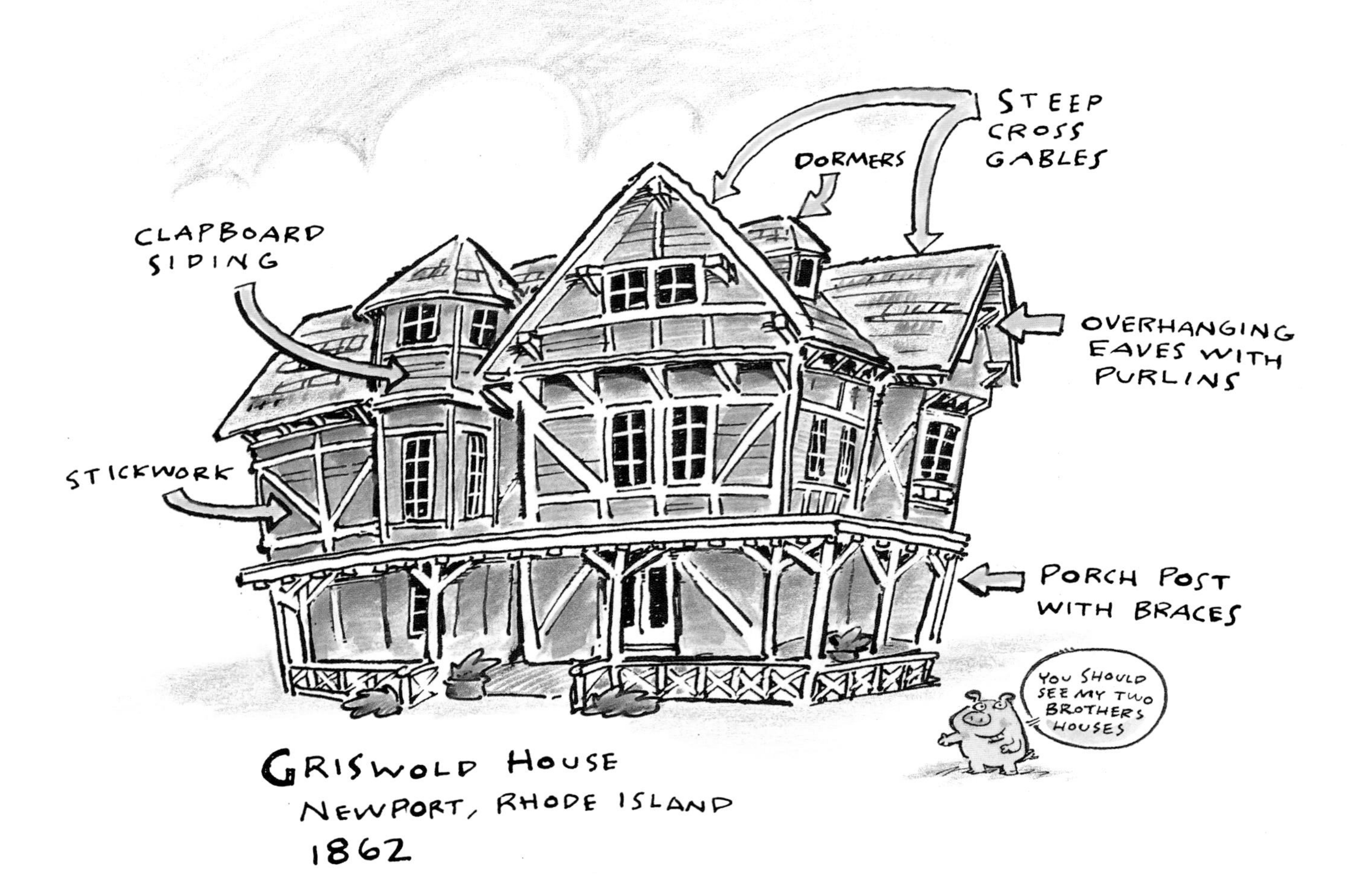

RICHARDSONIAN ROMANESQUE, 1870–1900

Richardsonian Romanesque takes its name from the architect Henry Hobson Richardson. This massive, heavy style uses masonry of rough-cut stone in several colors and sometimes brick laid in regular courses. The wide, round Romanesque arch framing the entryway is the key feature of the design.

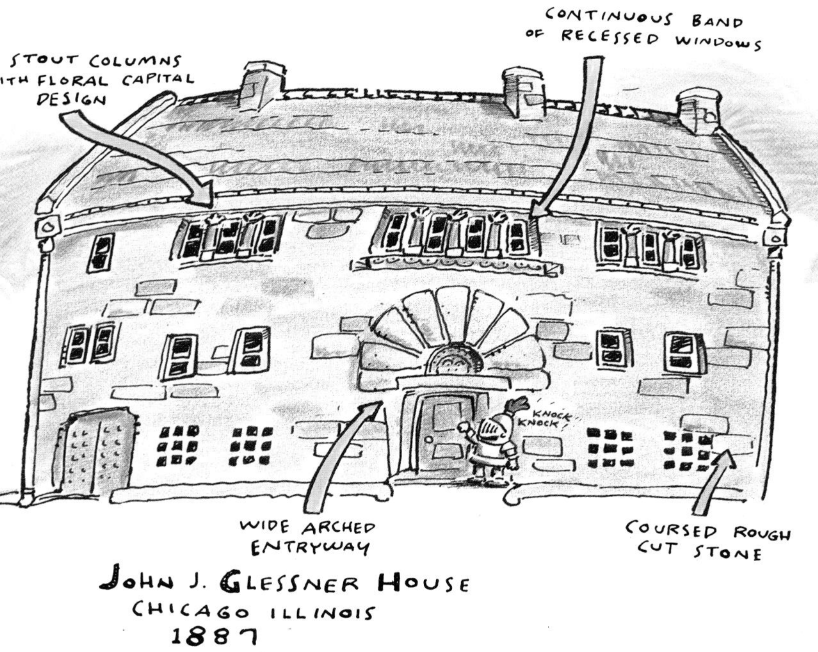

Windows are deeply recessed and often framed by small columns. Short towers with conical or pyramidal roofs are common. Another feature of this style is a loggia, an open gallery, behind colonnades at ground floor or higher up on the facade. The overall impression of the Richardsonian Romanesque is impressive and fortresslike.

QUEEN ANNE, 1880–1900

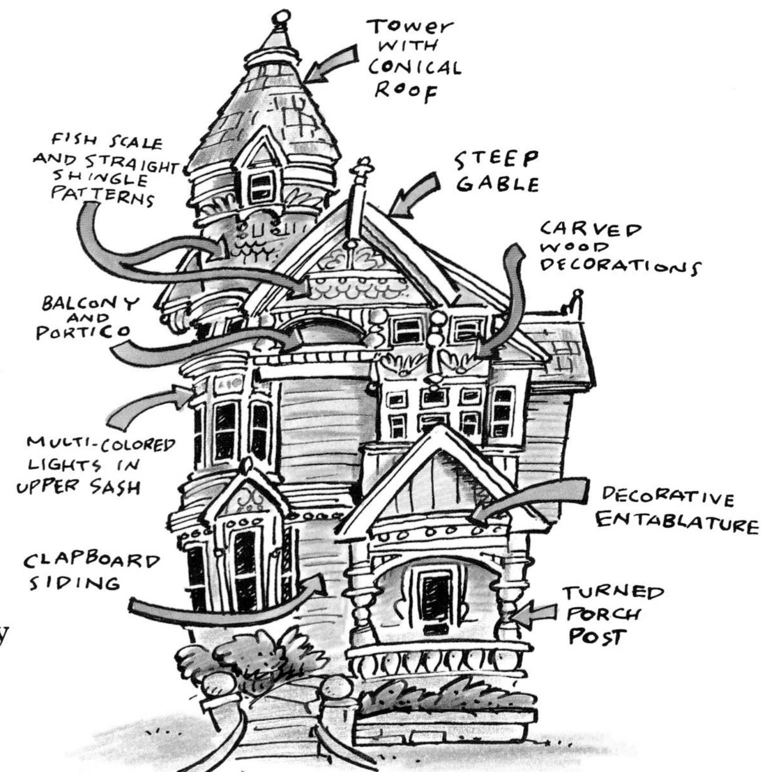

HAAS LILIENTHAL HOUSE
SAN FRANCISCO, CA.
1880

The Queen Anne Style, popularized in England by architect Richard Norman Shaw, was introduced into the United States in the last quarter of the 19th century. The style was enormously appealing. Pattern books and magazines provided floor plans, and factory-made woodcut architectural details could be ordered and transported across the country by train.

Queen Anne houses are often asymmetrical, with steep roofs, molded brick chimneys, towers, turrets, bay windows, balconies, porticos, and wide verandas. Borrowings from earlier styles account for the pediments, the classical columns, carved brackets, turned balustrades, swags, finials, and stickwork, which seem to cover every available space. Exterior walls are usually a combination of brick, stone, clapboard, decorative shingles, and stucco. Color and texture are key design elements. Wood and stucco surfaces and trim are painted in a range of complementary colors, and casement windows often feature tinted glass.

TYPICAL QUEEN ANNE COTTAGE
LATE 19th CENTURY

SHINGLE STYLE, 1880–1900

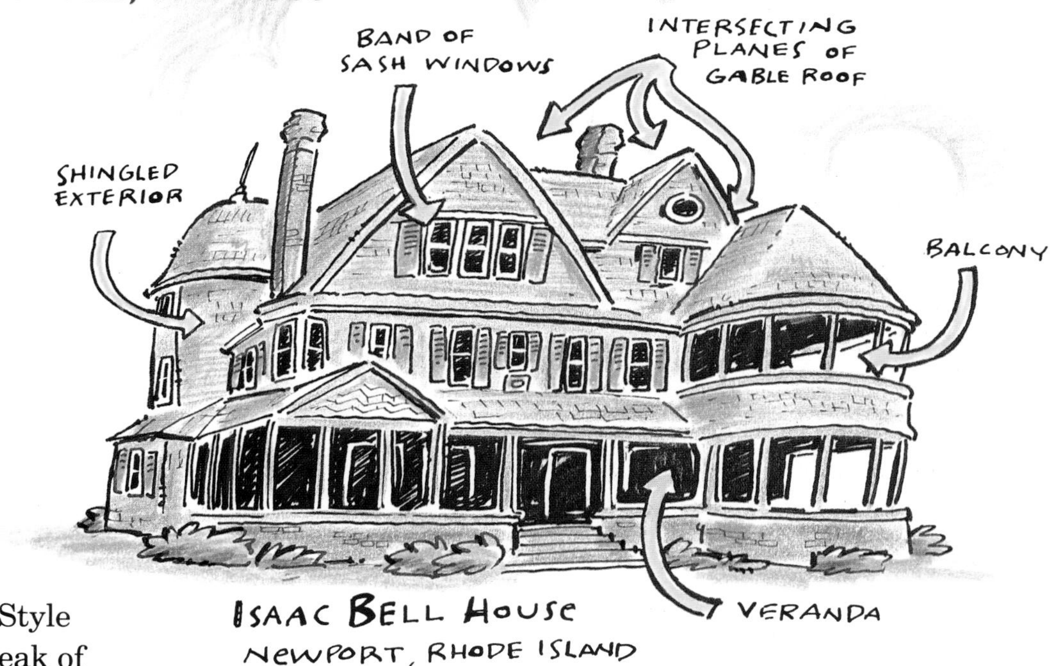

ISAAC BELL HOUSE
NEWPORT, RHODE ISLAND
1883

The Shingle Style reached its peak of popularity in New England. The style is recognized by the blanket of natural wood shingles covering the exterior walls from foundation to eaves. Bay windows, verandas, and balconies are common. Because they also are shingled, they seem more like bulges in the facade than separate features. There may also be towers, turrets, and dormers. Casement or sash windows are grouped in horizontal bands. The irregular profile of the roof line mirrors the rambling, swooping lines of the house. Columns or piers may be covered with shingles or built of rough-cut stone. Although the Shingle Style house owes much to Queen Anne design, the absence of ornament and the emphasis on natural color and materials allow for a simpler, less complex, and perhaps more welcoming home. Among the principal designers of the style were Henry Hobson Richardson; McKim, Mead and White; and Willis Polk.

VARIATION
LATE 19th CENTURY

SULLIVANESQUE/CHICAGO STYLE, 1890–1920

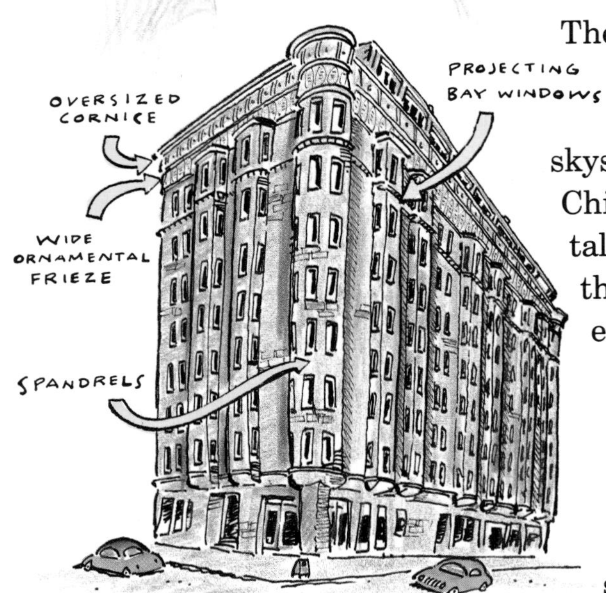

BREWSTER APARTMENT BUILDING.
CHICAGO, ILLINOIS
1893

The Chicago Style is also called the Commercial Style because it refers to high-rise commercial buildings. These early skyscrapers, the most notable of them built in Chicago, were between five and twenty stories tall. An underlying steel frame skeleton made this greater height possible by allowing the exterior walls of stone or brick to stretch like a skin over the structural frame of the building instead of actually supporting the walls of the building as they had in the past. For this reason a greater number of large windows could now be part of the outer wall surface.

The emphasis is on verticality with rectangular windows forming a horizontal grid. Bay windows running the full height of the building are common as are Chicago windows, a three-part window with a stationary central panel framed by narrow sashes. Large display windows are on the ground floor. The building is crowned by a heavy projecting cornice and flat roof. The style is distinguished by the wide band of intricate terra-cotta ornament decorating the frieze and often the spandrels and main entrance. The ornamentation is a unique blend of geometric and floral designs. The style was occasionally used for apartments.

Architect Louis Sullivan is most closely associated with this style. He designed so many Commercial Style buildings in Chicago that the style is often referred to as Sullivanesque or the Chicago Style. He is considered a pioneer in the art of the tall building, and the soaring glass boxes of today certainly depend on his early innovations.

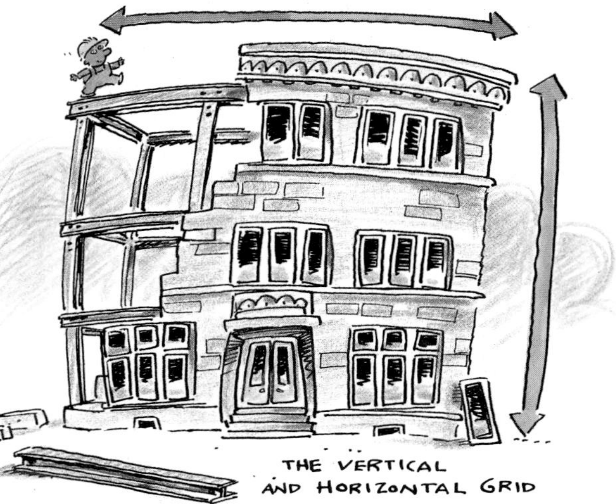

THE VERTICAL AND HORIZONTAL GRID

PRAIRIE STYLE 1900–1920

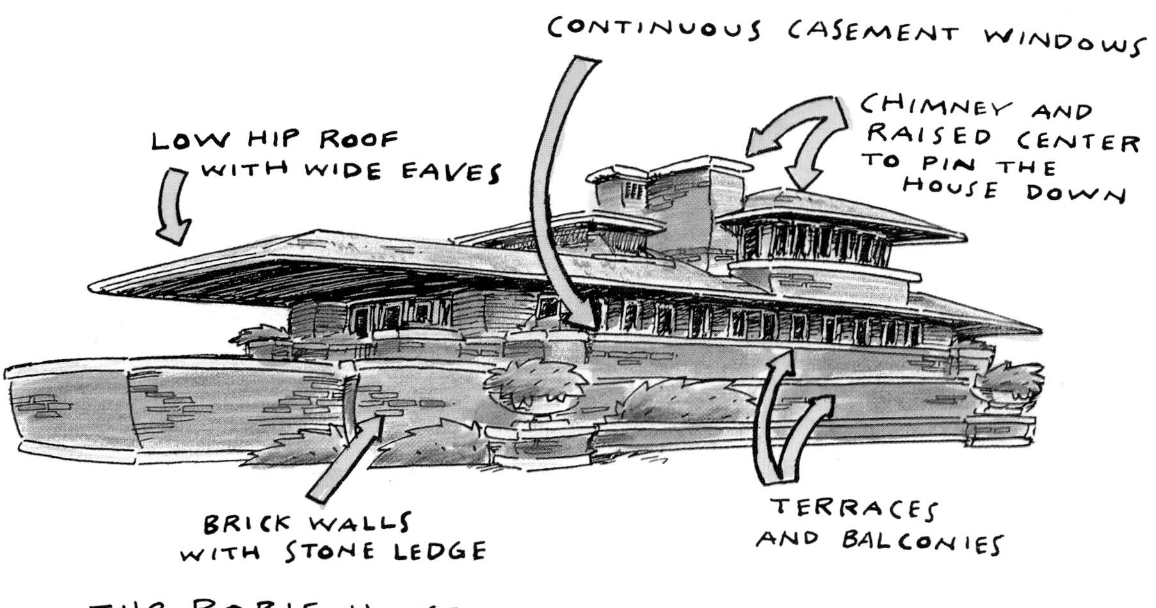

THE ROBIE HOUSE
CHICAGO, ILLINOIS
1909

The Prairie Style house is usually one to two stories high with a large chimney and slightly taller central section, which seems to pin the house to the ground. The horizontal lines of the house are emphasized by a low hip roof with wide eaves, long brick walls with stone ledges, and bands of casement windows tucked under the eaves and extending the length of the building. Terraces and balconies fan out from the center. Walls are built of brick or of timber covered with light-colored stucco.

WESTERN STICK STYLE OR CRAFTSMAN STYLE, 1890–1920

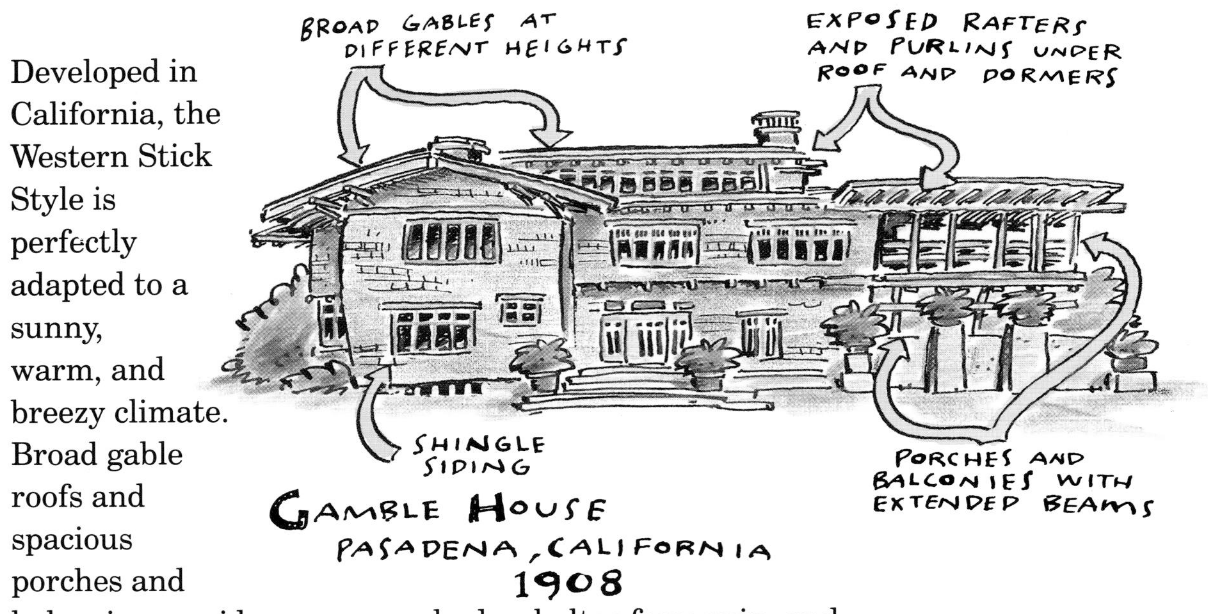

Developed in California, the Western Stick Style is perfectly adapted to a sunny, warm, and breezy climate. Broad gable roofs and spacious porches and balconies provide necessary shade, shelter from rain, and outdoor living space. The house is built on a horizontal axis (unlike the vertical Eastern Stick Style) and most typically of wood. Exposed rafters and purlins – sometimes shaped but often plain – extend well beyond the eaves of the gable or dormer roofs. The exposed wooden beams and framing elements of balconies, porches, and porticos around windows have a "stick style" appearance and seem to fit snugly together like the pieces of a puzzle. The exterior wall surfaces are generally clapboard or shingle.

The Western Stick Style or Craftsman Style was popularized in California by the architectural team of Greene and Greene. Their common sense design and simple, natural materials shaped the Bungalow Style, whose popularity was spread through magazines, pattern books, and mail order catalogues. Variations of this style are everywhere.

SPANISH COLONIAL REVIVAL, 1890–1940

A renewed interest in Spanish architectural traditions around the turn of the century led to an imaginative revival style in the Southern part of the United States. The two-story homes in this style have stuccoed exteriors and low-pitched red tile roofs. The central feature is the entryway which, at its most elaborate, is surrounded by pilasters, spiral columns, decorative tiles, and carved crests or sculptural relief. More modest houses have wooden doors. Arched windows, doorways, and arcades are common, but so are straight-headed openings and loggias. Windows are often enclosed by ornamental wrought iron grills or carved wooden balustrades; balconies have railings of the same materials. Towers and chimneys are capped by small tile roofs. House plans vary in shape, with exterior stairways or entryways leading to a rear garden or patio. The work of architect Addison Mizner is closely associated with the Spanish Colonial Revival Style, and his homes along the Florida coast are among its finest examples.

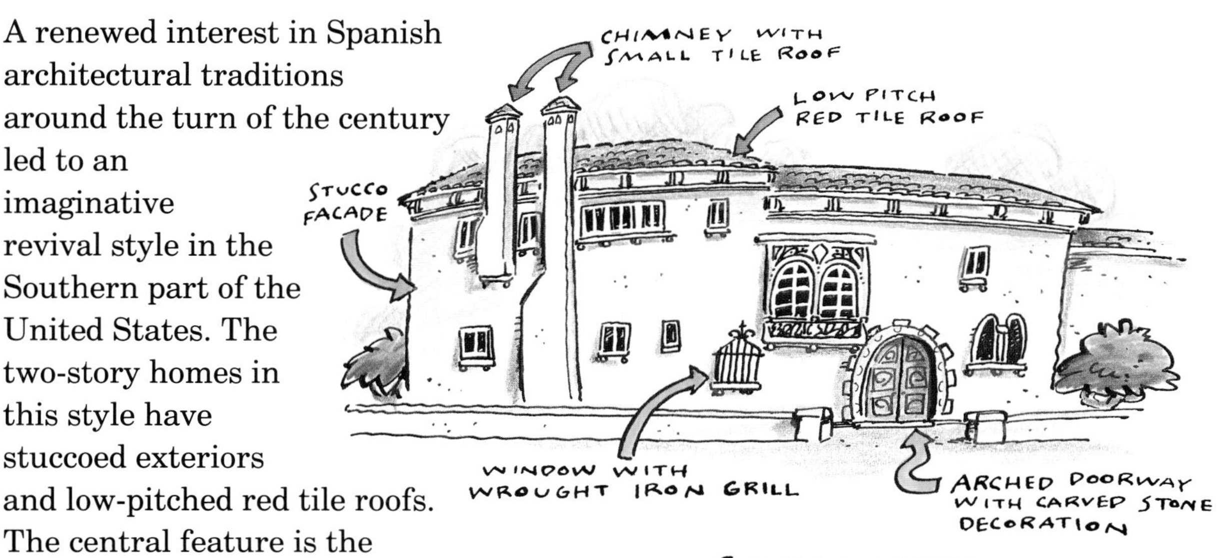

WILLIAM GRAY WARDEN HOUSE
PALM BEACH FLORIDA - 1922

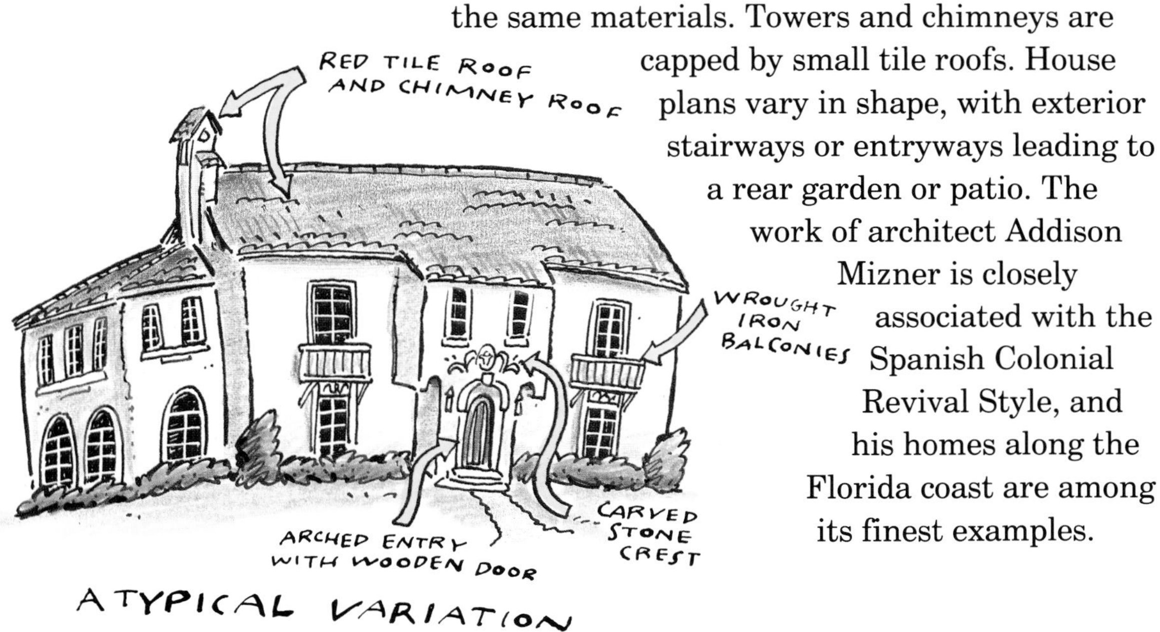

A TYPICAL VARIATION

MODERNISTIC, 1925–45

The modernistic styles of Art Deco and Art Moderne were for the most part a form of decoration. Inspired by the European Exposition des Artes Décoratifs held in Paris in 1925, Americans began to abandon historical revival styles in favor of this new modern movement.

ART DECO, 1925–40

MCGAY RESIDENCE
TULSA, OKLAHOMA
1936

The Art Deco period is the earliest example of modernism. It is best characterized by a linear, hard-edged ornamentation applied to a smooth concrete, stucco, or stone wall surface. Designs are of zigzag, geometric, floral motifs, or linear patterns in low relief. This relief frames doorways and windows and is applied around roof edges and along the parapet. Colored glass, glazed bricks, and even colored ceramic are used for effect. In general, Art Deco was preferred for commercial structures and apartment buildings with an emphasis on verticality. Setbacks near the roof line are typical. Art Deco is less common for residential architecture, but some fine examples do exist.

ART MODERNE, 1930–45

Streamlined is the best way to describe Art Moderne architecture. Influenced by automobile, airplane, and ship designs, the look has curved wall surfaces, aluminum trim for windows and doorways, and sleek bands of windows that wrap around corners and run like ribbons across the facade. Ornament is kept to a minimum – simple panels of low relief – and cement or stucco buildings are painted in pale tones. Doors are metal or wood and often have porthole windows. Art Moderne was a very popular style for apartment buildings but less favored for private houses.

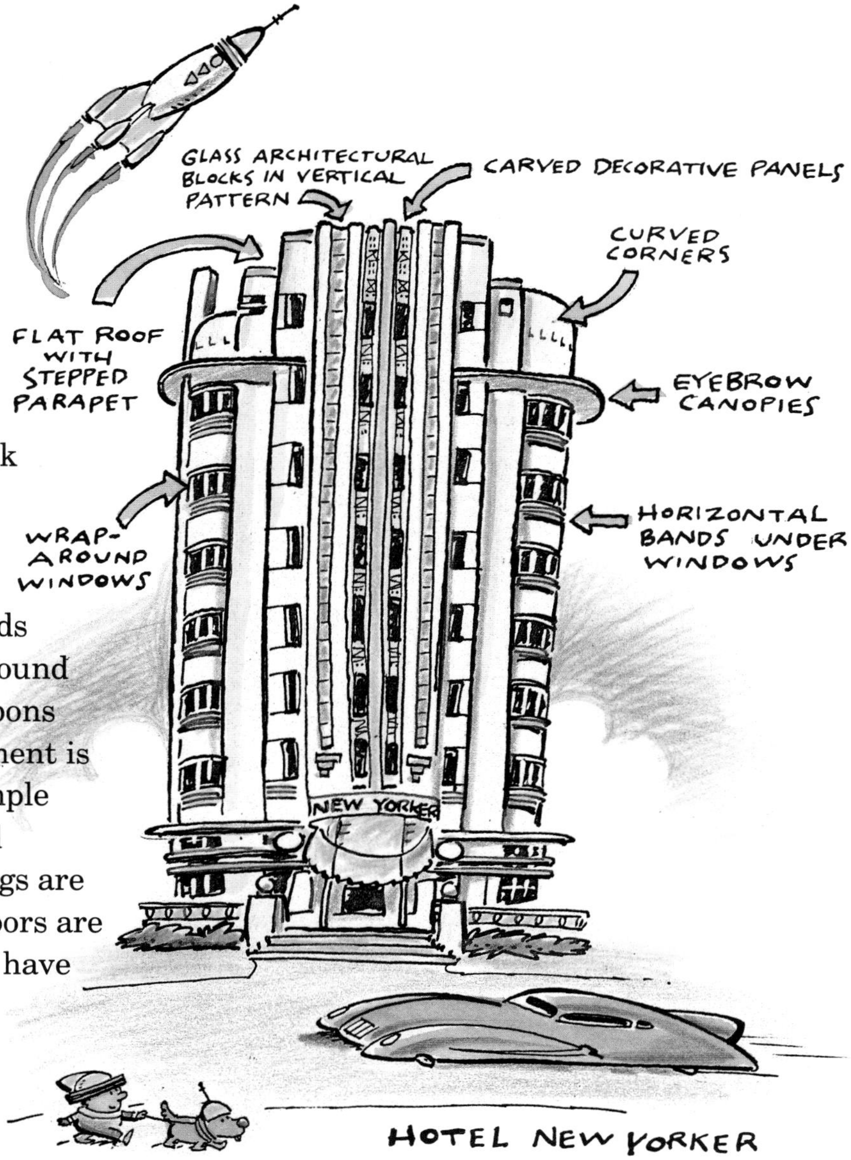

HOTEL NEW YORKER
MIAMI BEACH, FLORIDA
1940

HOTEL NEW YORKER – AS IT LOOKS TODAY

INTERNATIONAL STYLE, 1920–present

In 1932 the Museum of Modern Art had its first exhibition of architecture. Photographs and drawings by architects all around the globe were displayed. Historian Henry-Russell Hitchcock and architect Philip Johnson wrote the book for the show, entitled *The International Style: Architecture Since 1932*. Through their definition and name for it, the style became widely known, accepted, and practiced. Architects fleeing Europe during World War II began working in the United States and teaching at American universities. Their influence was profound, and their work laid the foundation for modern architecture as we know it today.

Le Corbusier said a house is "a machine for living." By that he meant that a house should above all be functional, not decorative, and should meet the daily needs of the inhabitants. The International Style attempted to do just that. It is certainly without ornament. The plain white stucco or concrete walls are interrupted only by bands of ribbon windows that are flush with the wall surface. Often windows form the corner of the building, reemphasizing that they are merely part of the fabric of the wall surface. In other places, large floor-to-ceiling panes of glass form part of the exterior walls. Roofs are flat and have no eaves. The basic plan of the house is asymmetrical, with cantilevered balconies and portions of the roof or even entire floors extending out from the central mass. Frequently heavy pillars or piloti support the ground floor, giving the impression that the house itself hovers above the ground.

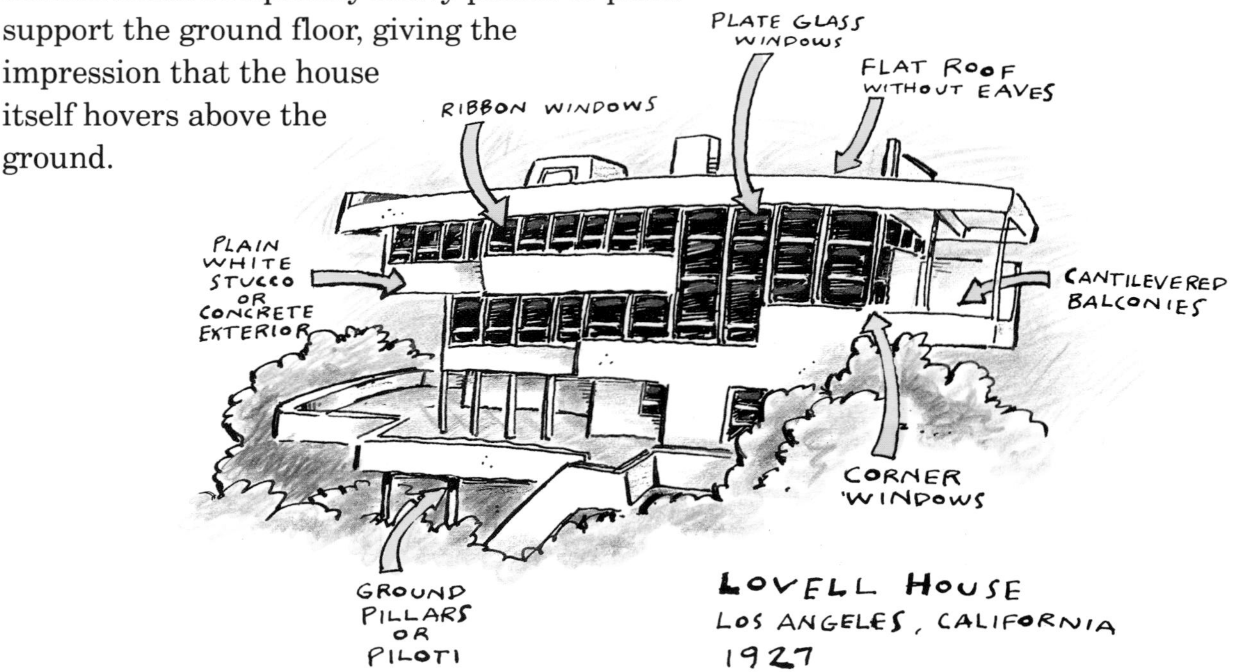

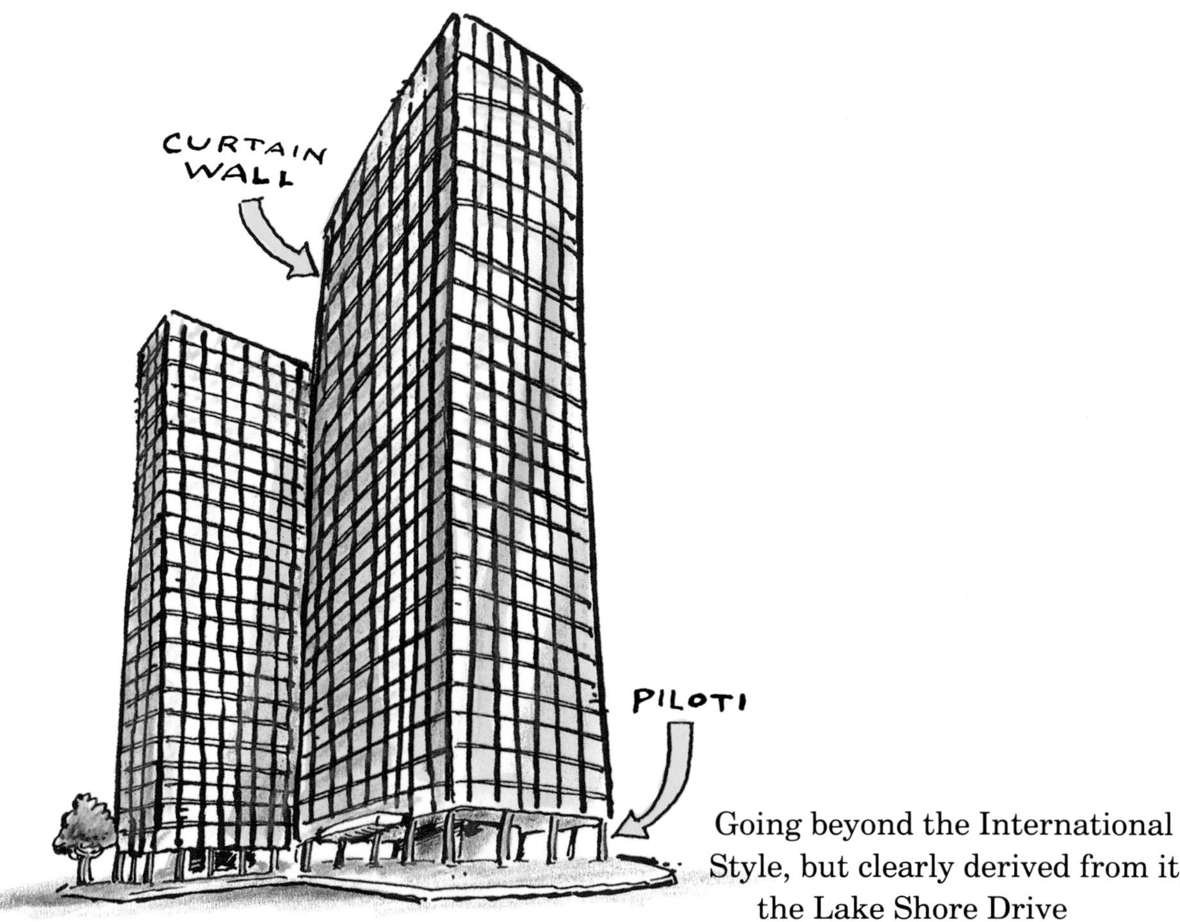

Going beyond the International Style, but clearly derived from it, the Lake Shore Drive apartments in Chicago exhibit a similar "function first" approach. These buildings were designed by Ludwig Mies van der Rohe. He emphasized structural simplicity, curtain-wall construction in which the windows are part of the wall surface, supporting piloti to emphasize volume, not weight, and total lack of ornament. The ideas of Louis Sullivan's skyscraper are fully realized here in the emphatic verticality and exposed steel-frame skeleton. This type of building and others that follow it push construction materials and building technology to their absolute limits to create ever more exiting and challenging architecture.

UP TO THE PRESENT AND BEYOND, 1945–present

After World War II, returning servicemen and their families were eager to have homes of their own. They didn't have much money, so the houses, for the most part, were more modest in size and simpler in design than those of the prewar years. Builders took earlier historical styles as a pattern, using various design elements in combination or alone to give new life to once popular styles or to create new types of suburban dwellings.

Although the Bungalow reached its peak of popularity in the 1920s, it has always been favored as a housing type. Usually one to one-and-a-half stories high, the Bungalow has a broad gable roof with wide eaves, a spacious front porch with supporting piers or columns, and a prominent chimney. Exterior walls are of brick, stone, wood, or stucco. The house can adapt to any number of historical styles; most often it is Classical, Colonial, or Craftsman.

AMERICAN FOURSQUARE

The American Foursquare can be thought of as a mixture of Bungalow, Prairie, and Colonial Revival Style houses. Typically two to two-and-a-half stories tall, this house has a foundation, a chimney, and a porch with supporting piers, all constructed from brick or stone. Upper walls are usually clad with wood or stucco. The roof is hip or gable with wide overhangs. Dormers or gable-end windows illuminate the attic space. Large sash windows are tucked under the eaves.

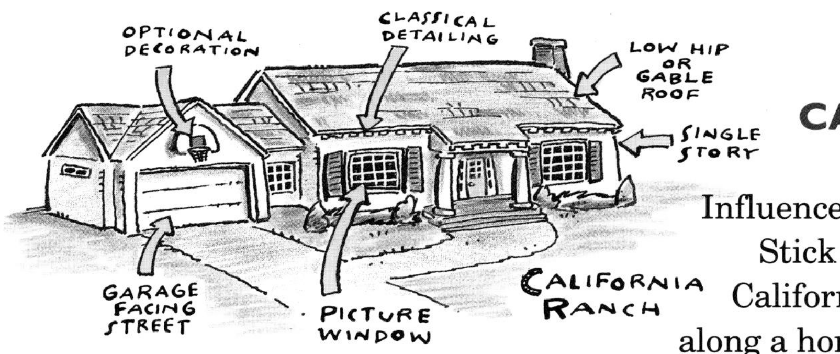

CALIFORNIA RANCH

Influenced by Prairie and Western Stick styles, the one-story California Ranch stretches itself along a horizontal axis. Larger lot sizes allow for a wider facade that includes the garage on the side facing the street. Home sizes vary from quite small to spacious and rambling. Large picture windows on the front of the home are common, as are sliding-glass doors leading to the patio at the rear. Low-pitched roofs are hipped or gabled. Exterior walls are commonly of brick and wood, with modest Colonial or Classical detailing.

SPLIT LEVEL

LOW PITCH ROOF (HIP-GABLE OR BOTH)
SPLIT DOUBLE STORY
WOOD SIDING
PICTURE WINDOW
SPLIT LEVEL

The Split Level, introduced in the 1950s, is one of the most versatile and popular suburban homes. Three levels accommodate a family entertainment area, kitchen and dining room areas, and sleeping areas. The entrance leads into the living room, and a short flight of stairs leads up or down to other rooms in the two-story portion of the house. A wide facade with picture window and a low-pitched gable or hip roof give the Split Level a look similar to the Ranch. The Split Level is often decorated with shutters and wrought iron railings.

COTSWOLD COTTAGE

Among the revival styles, the Cotswold Cottage is particularly popular, appearing again and again with slight variations in neighborhoods everywhere. The style is characterized by an oversized brick or stone chimney on the front or side of the house; a steep gable roof; casement windows, often with leaded glass; dormer windows; and exterior walls of brick, stone, and stucco with half timbering. The overall effect is comfortable and quaint.

NEO-EXPRESSIONISM

Neo-Expressionism comes closer to sculpture than perhaps any other housing form. Here the architect, completely freed from historical styles, can use any construction techniques, materials, and designs for expressive effect. The aim is to create, in three-dimensional form, the essential idea behind the structure. In this way the construction takes on a dramatic quality that communicates its own unique meaning through its own singular form.

Arcosanti, an architectural complex Paolo Soleri designed in Arizona, is a fine example of Neo-Expressionist architecture. The buildings seem shaped more than constructed, with a preference for shell-like vaults and rounded forms. One of the techniques Soleri used was to reinforce mounds of earth or river silt, then cover them with concrete or gunite. Later when the concrete had dried, the earth was scooped out, leaving a hollow vault that created some unusual forms. Color, added here and there, adds visual interest in the small community.

"SCOOPED OUT" AREA SHELTER
WORK BENCH
ROCKS

PART THREE

FIELD GUIDE

Use this Field Guide to help you look at the houses in your neighborhood and determine their style. Examine one house at a time. Study the illustrations in each category on the following pages and locate the architectural features that most closely resemble the building you are investigating. Carry a pad of paper and pencil with you out into the field. Sketch what you see, and then label the parts.

If most of the features you find on your structure fit within a style category outlined in the previous section – identify your house style! If some but not all of the features appear on your house, then most likely you have a regional variation of that style. If the architectural features of your house don't follow a particular style pattern, or if you see something not shown here, then you are probably looking at vernacular or folk housing unique to your part of the country.

Be on the lookout for alterations or additions to the original house. Such changes can give you false data about the building, making it hard to pinpoint a date or a style.

To see how the Field Guide really works, let's check out the designs of different houses.

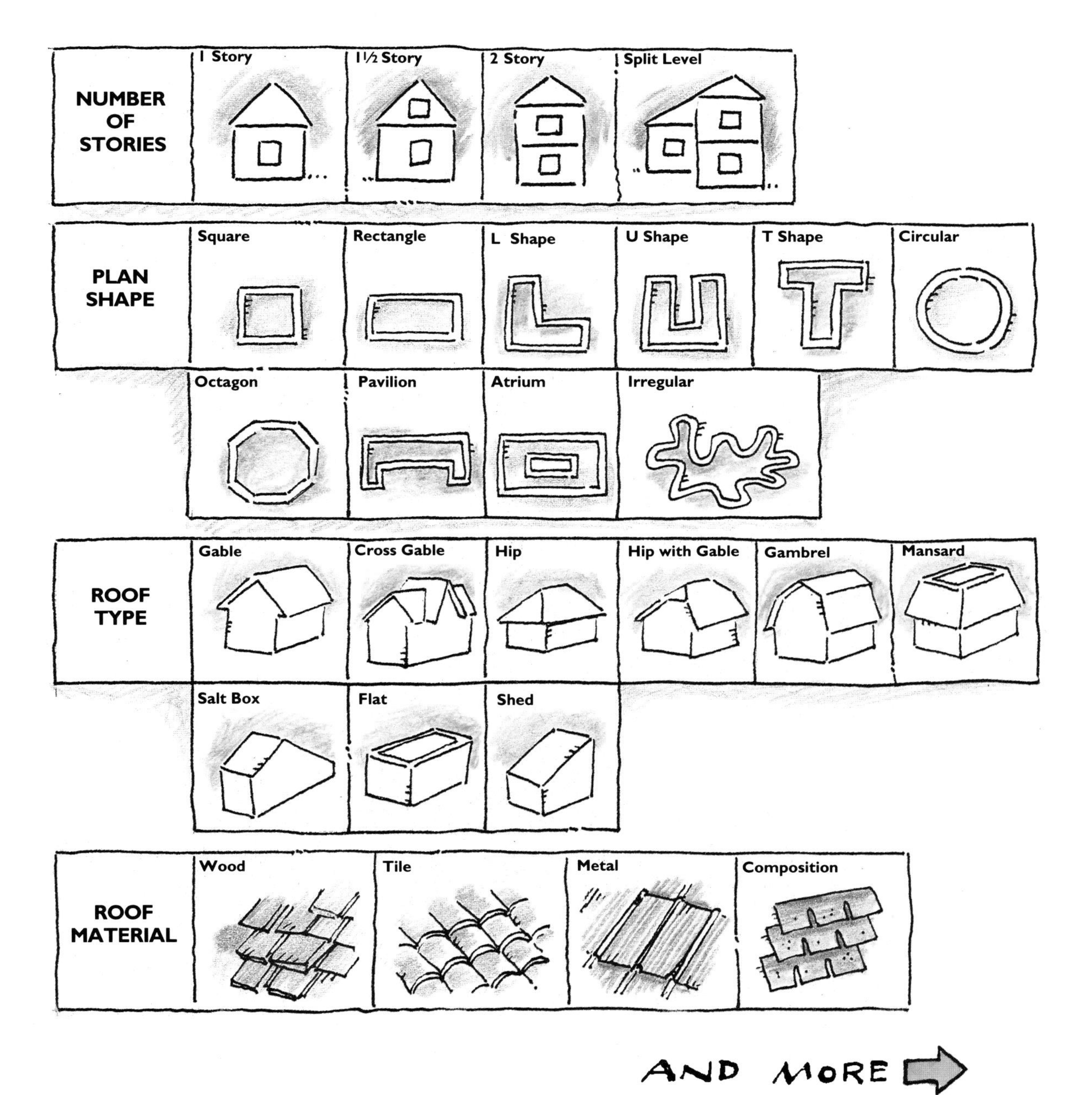
NUMBER OF STORIES
1 Story
1½ Story
2 Story
Split Level
PLAN SHAPE
Square
Rectangle
L Shape
U Shape
T Shape
Circular
Octagon
Pavilion
Atrium
Irregular
ROOF TYPE
Gable
Cross Gable
Hip
Hip with Gable
Gambrel
Mansard
Salt Box
Flat
Shed
ROOF MATERIAL
Wood
Tile
Metal
Composition
AND MORE

THIS IS A CARPENTER GOTHIC STYLE HOME— WHAT ARE ITS DISTINCTIVE FEATURES?

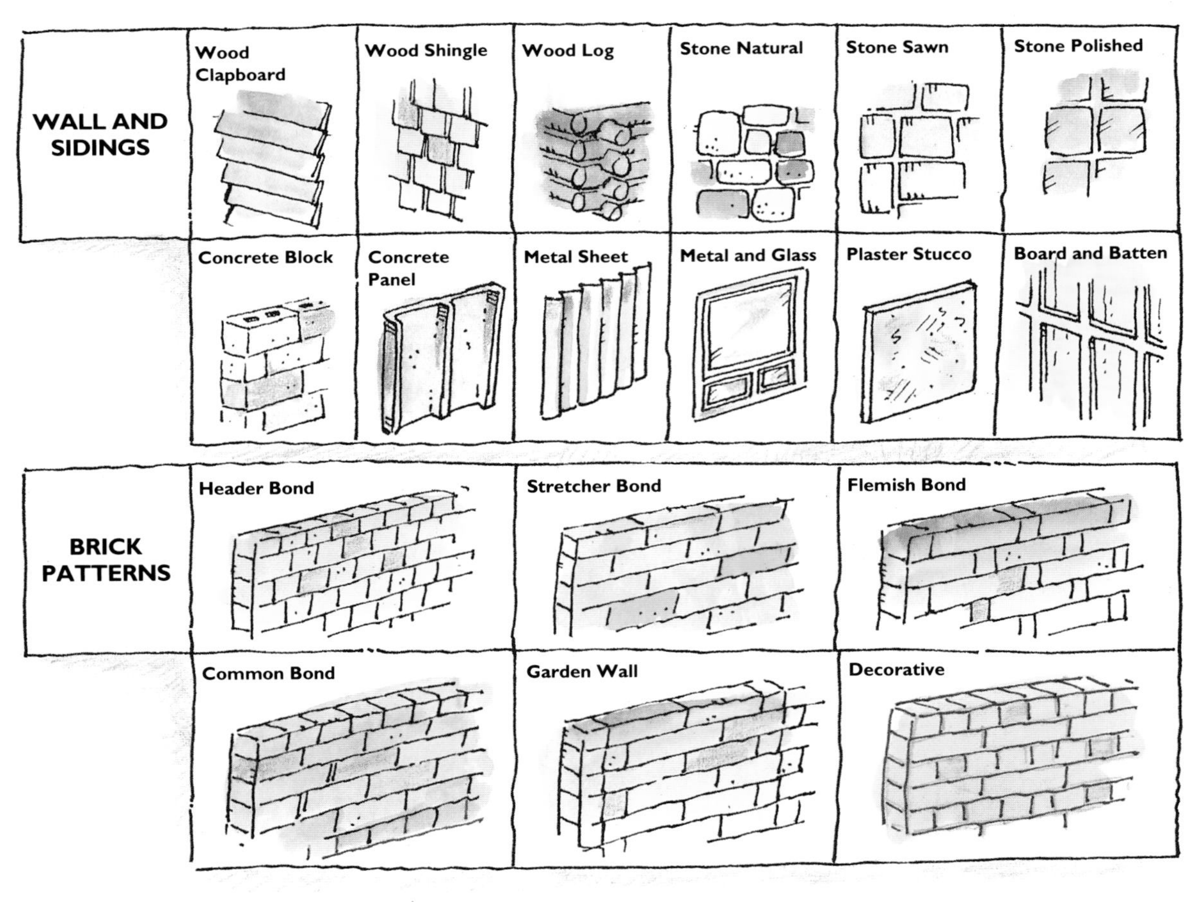

AND MORE and MORE

• CAN YOU IDENTIFY THE STYLE OF THIS HOUSE? (LOOK BACK INTO THE STYLE GUIDE)
• USING THE CHARTS IN THIS SECTION, WHAT OTHER FEATURES CAN YOU IDENTIFY?
DECORATIVE MOLDED BRICK CHIMNEY
FISH SCALE SHINGLE PATTERNS
CARVED WOODEN BRACKETS AND ORNAMENTS
NATURAL STONE FOUNDATION
WOOD CLAPBOARD SIDING

DOUBLE-HUNG WINDOWS
DENTILS
PILASTERS
GEORGIAN STYLE
TRANSOM
PEDIMENT
SIDE-LIGHTS
ADAM STYLE
CASEMENT WINDOWS
PLASTER/STUCCO
WOM
GLASS BLOCKS
ART MODERNE STYLE

WHAT KIND OF WINDOWS DOES IT HAVE?
WHAT TYPE OF ROOF IS THAT?
DOES IT HAVE A PORCH?
WHAT ABOUT THE FLOOR PLAN?

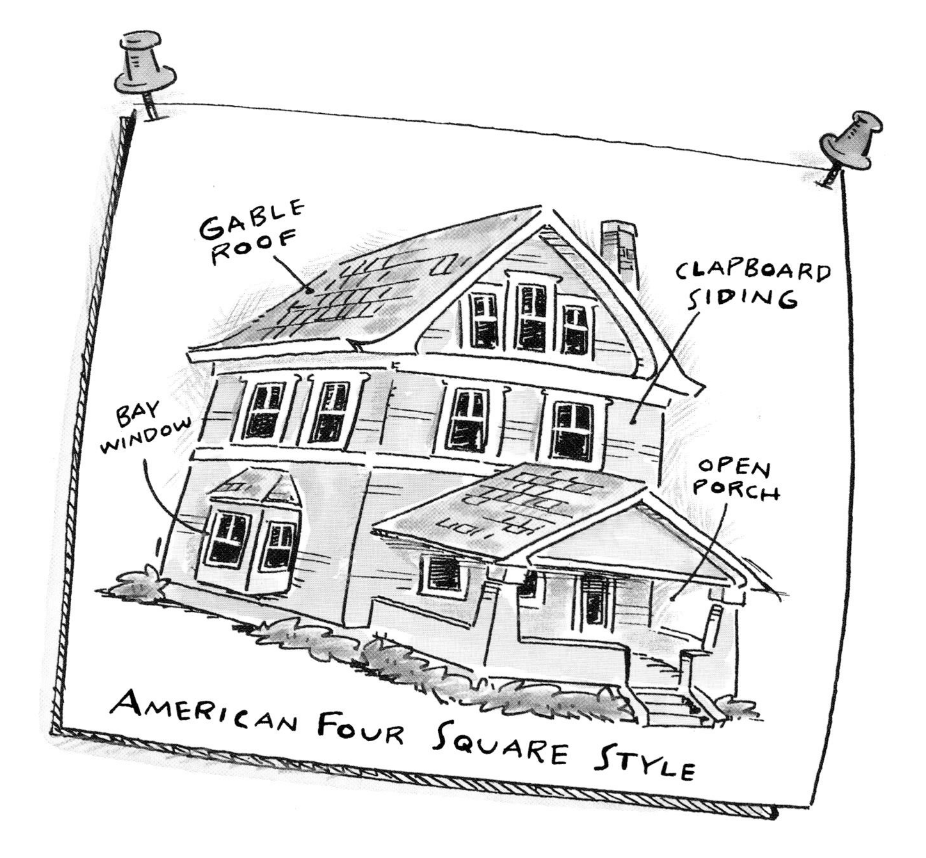
GABLE ROOF
CLAPBOARD SIDING
BAY WINDOW
OPEN PORCH
AMERICAN FOUR SQUARE STYLE

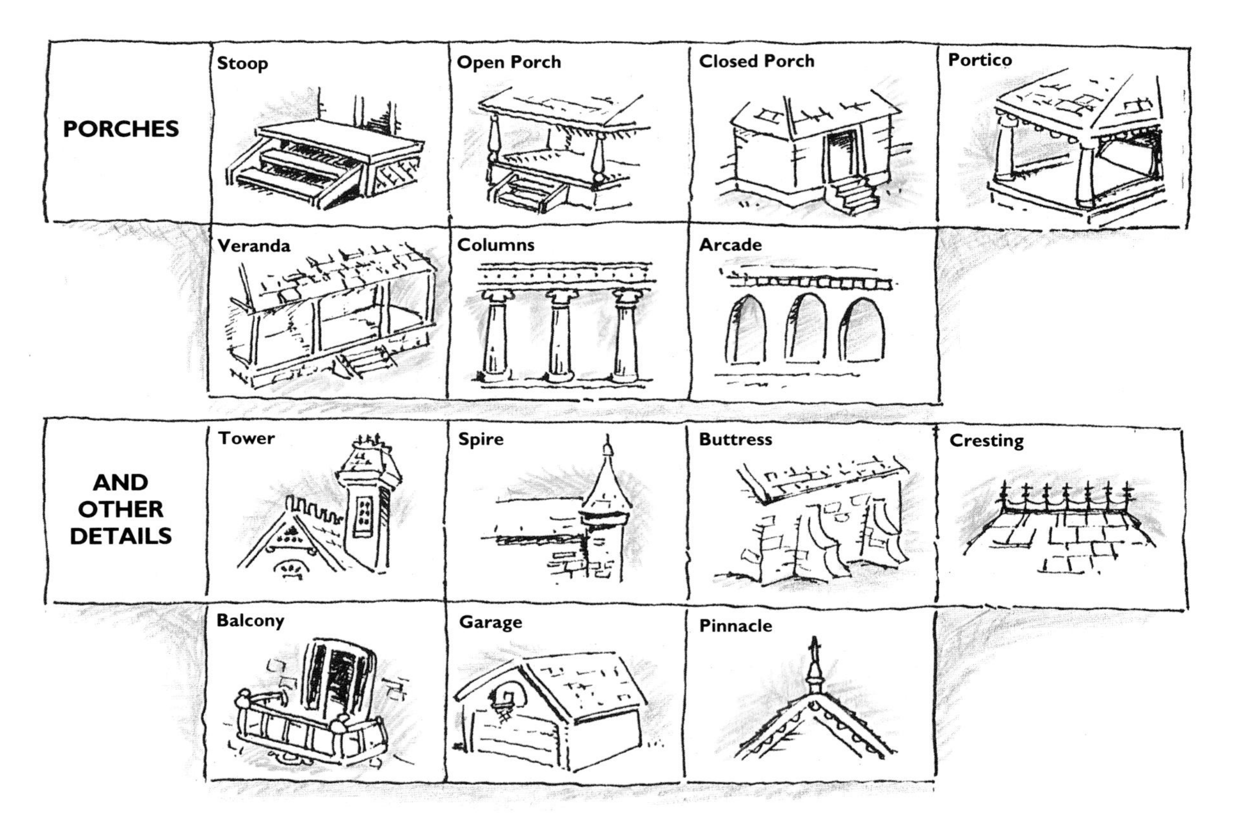
PORCHES
Stoop
Open Porch
Closed Porch
Portico
Veranda
Columns
Arcade
AND OTHER DETAILS
Tower
Spire
Buttress
Cresting
Balcony
Garage
Pinnacle

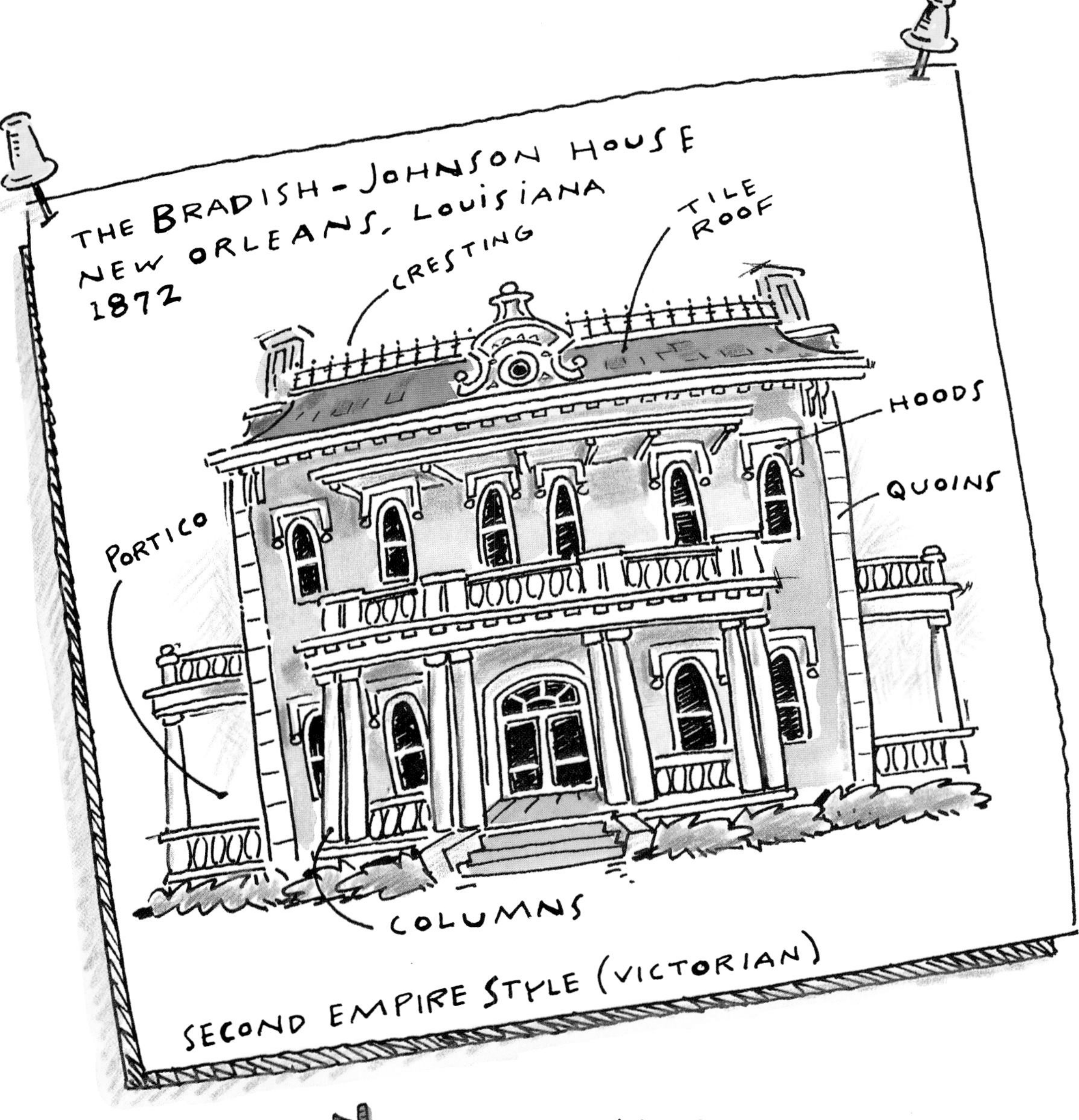

NOW YOU HAVE IT ALL— BY USING THE FIELD and STYLE GUIDES IN THIS BOOK YOU CAN IDENTIFY ANY HOUSE.

START BY SKETCHING YOUR HOME.

PART FOUR

LOCATION, HISTORIC STATUS, AND ACCESSIBILITY

Page	Historic Status	Location, Architect, and Accessibility to Public
10-11	*National Register*	Boswell Ranch, Laramie, Wyoming. Late 19th century. Privately owned. Not accessible.
12, 66	*National Register*	Palace of the Governors, Santa Fe, New Mexico. c. 1610. Restored to its early 19th century appearance. Operated by Museum of New Mexico Foundation. Open daily.
13, 76	*National Register*	Oak Alley Plantation, Vacherie, Louisiana. Joseph Pilie, architect, 1830-36. Owned and operated by Oak Alley Foundation. Open daily.
15	*National Register*	Cliff Palace, Mesa Verde National Park, Cortez, Colorado. c. 1220. Operated by the National Park Service. Open daily.
15	*National Register*	Clan House, Totem Bight Historic Park, Ketchikan, Alaska. Operated by Alaska State Parks. Open daily.
17	*National Register*	William R. Dowse House, Custer County, Nebraska. William R. Dowse, builder, c. 1900. Privately owned. Open daily.
19, 64	*National Register*	Jethro Coffin House, Nantucket Island, Massachusetts. Late 17th century. Owned and operated by the Nantucket Historical Association. Open seasonally.
20, 68	*National Register*	Abraham Yates House, Stockade Historic District, Schenectady, New York. Early 18th century.
21	*National Register*	John Dickinson House, Salem County, Alloway vicinity, New Jersey. Built by "DIM," 1754. There have been alterations. Privately owned. Not accessible.
21	*National Register*	Hans Herr House, Lancaster, Pennsylvania. Christian Herr, architect. 1719. Operated by the Lancaster Mennonite Historical Society, Lancaster County, Pennsylvania. Open daily.

Page	Historic Status	Location, Architect, and Accessibility to Public
22, 71	*National Register*	Monticello, Charlottesville, Virginia. Thomas Jefferson, architect. 1768-92;1793-1809. Owned and operated by the Thomas Jefferson Memorial Foundation. Open daily.
23		Philip Johnson House, New Canaan, Connecticut. Philip Johnson, architect. 1949.
24-25, 75	*National Register*	Longwood or "Nutt's Folly," Natchez, Mississippi. Samuel Sloan, architect. 1860-62. Owned and operated by Pilgrimage Garden Club of Natchez, Mississippi. Open daily.
26-27	*Local Register*	712-722 Steiner, Alamo Square Neighborhood, San Francisco, California. Late 19th century.
30-31	*National Register*	Biltmore Estate, Asheville, North Carolina. Richard Morris Hunt, architect. 1890-95. Privately owned. Open daily.
32-33	*National Register*	Wilhelm Pelster House Barn, South Haven, Missouri. c. 1860. Department of Natural Resources, Historic Preservation Revolving Fund Program, State of Missouri. Not open.
34	*Local Register and National Register*	Ball House, King William Historic District, San Antonio, Texas. 1868.
34	*National Register*	2325 Constance, Irish Channel Historic District, New Orleans, Louisiana. Mid-19th century.
35	*Local Register*	Daniel G. Hughes Cabin, Clay County Historic District, Shoal Creek, Missouri.1825-30. Owned and operated by the City of Kansas City Parks and Recreation. Accessible for exterior view and by appointment.
35	*National Register*	321 South Lee Street, Alexandria Historic District, Alexandria, Virginia. c. 1824.

Page	Historic Status	Location, Architect, and Accessibility to Public
36		Alta Mining Camp, Colorado Rockies. Late 19th century.
37	*National Register*	Colorado Avenue, Telluride National Historic Landmark District, Telluride, Colorado. c. 1875.
38	*National Register*	Paul Revere House, Boston, Massachusetts. 1680. Owned and operated by Paul Revere Memorial Association. Open daily.
38	*National Register*	The Ingalls Home on Third Street, 210 3rd Street, De Smet, South Dakota. Owned and Operated by Laura Ingalls Wilder Memorial Society. Open seasonally.
39	*National Register*	Charles A. Lindbergh House, Little Falls, Minnesota. 1906. Owned and operated by the Minnesota Historical Society. Open seasonally.
39	*National Register*	`Iolani Palace, Honolulu, Hawaii, 1882. Operated by the Friends of `Iolani Palace. Open daily and by appointment.
40-41, 70	*National Register*	The White House, Washington, D.C., James Hoban, architect. 1792-1829. Operated by the National Park Service. Open daily.
43, 83	*National Register*	Frederick C. Robie House, Chicago, Illinois, Frank Lloyd Wright, architect. 1909. Owned and operated by the University of Chicago. Open daily for noon tours and for special tours by appointment.
46	*National Register*	Kansas City Porch Apartment, Santa Fe Place Historic District, Kansas City, Missouri. Early 20th century. Privately owned. Not accessible.
46, 89	*National Register*	860-880 North Lake Shore Drive, Chicago, Illinois. Mies van der Rohe, architect. 1945-51. Privately owned. Not accessible.
47		Atrium on the Plaza. 4577-4589 Walnut, Kansas City, Missouri. Moshe Safdie, architect. 1980. Privately owned. Not accessible.

Page	Historic Status	Location, Architect, and Accessibility to Public
48	*Local Register and National Register*	Brownstones, Brooklyn Heights Historic District, Brooklyn, New York. 1852-60. Privately owned. Not accessible.
49	*National Register*	Row Houses, Hyde Park/Kenwood Historic District, Chicago, Illinois. c. 1988. Privately owned. Not accessible.
49	*National Register*	Gartz Court, Pasadena, California. Attributable to Myron Hunt and Elmer Grey. 1910. Privately owned. Not accessible.
50		Dymaxion II, Beech Aircraft Co. R. Buckminster Fuller, architect. 1944.
51		Buckminster Fuller House, Carbondale, Illinois. Buckminster Fuller, architect. 1960. Privately owned. Not accessible.
56	*National Register*	Lucy the Elephant, Margate, New Jersey. James V. Lafferty, architect. 1881. Privately owned. Open daily.
56		Earthship, Taos, New Mexico. Michael Reynolds, architect. Privately owned. Not accessible.
57	*National Register*	The Haines Shoe House, Hallam, Pennsylvania. Mahlon Haines, architect. 1949. Privately owned. Open by appointment only.
57		The James Nicol House, Kansas City, Missouri. Bruce Goff, architect. 1966-67. Privately owned. Not accessible.
58-59, 92-93		Arcosanti, near Cordes Junction, Arizona. Paolo Soleri, architect. Begun 1950s. Privately owned.
60		Charleston Cottages, Charleston, South Carolina. Christopher Rose, architect. 1991. Privately owned. Not accessible.
61		"City Sleeper" and "Starter Home." Donald MacDonald, architect.

Page	Historic Status	Location, Architect, and Accessibility to Public
62	*National Register*	Drayton Hall, Charleston, South Carolina. 1738-42. Owned and operated by the National Trust for Historic Preservation. Open daily.
63	*National Register*	Frank Lloyd Wright Home and Studio, Oak Park, Illinois. Frank Lloyd Wright, architect. 1889, 1898. Owned by the National Trust for Historic Preservation. Operated by Frank Lloyd Wright Home and Studio Foundation. Open daily.
63	*National Register*	Horace Baker Log Cabin, Oregon City, Oregon. Horace Baker, architect. 1856. Owned and operated by Baker Cabin Historical Society. Open by appointment only.
65	*National Register*	Bacon's Castle, Surry County, Virginia. 1665. Owned and operated for the Preservation of Virginia Antiquities. Open seasonally.
66	*National Register*	Casa Amesti, Monterey, California. c.1834, 1846. Owned by the National Trust for Historic Preservation. Open daily.
67	*National Register*	Jean-Baptiste Saucier House (Cahokia Courthouse), Cahokia, Illinois. 1737. Owned and operated by the State of Illinois Historic Preservation Agency. Open on a limited basis.
67	*National Register*	Homeplace Plantation, Hahnville, Louisiana. 19th century. Privately owned. Open by appointment.
68	*National Register*	Lefferts Homestead, Brooklyn, New York. c. 1783. Owned by New York City Department of Parks and Recreation. Operated by Prospect Park Alliance as a Children's Historic House Museum. Open seasonally by appointment.
69	*National Register*	Cliveden, Philadelphia, Pennsylvania. 1763-67. Owned by the National Trust for Historic Preservation. Operated by Cliveden, Inc. Open daily.
69	*National Register*	Mount Pleasant, Fairmount Park, Philadelphia, Pennsylvania. Thomas Newell, carpenter. 1762 - 65. Owned and operated by the City of Philadelphia as part of Fairmount Park.

Page	Historic Status	Location, Architect, and Accessibility to Public
70	*National Register*	Decatur House, Washington, D.C. Benjamin Latrobe, architect. 1819. Owned and operated by the National Trust for Historic Preservation. Open daily.
71	*National Register*	Belle Grove, Middletown, Virginia. 1794. Owned by the National Trust for Historic Preservation. Operated by Belle Grove, Inc. Open daily.
72	*National Register*	Andalusia, Bucks County, Pennsylvania. 1836. Privately owned. Open by appointment only to groups.
73	*National Register*	Lyndhurst, Tarrytown, New York. 1838-64. Owned and operated by the National Trust for Historic Preservation. Open seasonally on a limited basis.
74	*National Register*	Frederick Hall House (Hall-Fowler Memorial Library), Ionia, Michigan. Captain Lucius Mills, architect/builder. Owned and operated by the City of Ionia. Open daily.
76	*National Register*	Woodrow Wilson House, Washington, D.C. 1915. Owned and operated by the National Trust for Historic Preservation. Open daily.
77	*State Register and National Register*	Gallatin House (Governor's Mansion), Sacramento, California. Nathaniel Goodell, architect. 1877-78. Owned and operated by the California Department of Parks and Recreation. Open daily.
78	*National Register*	J.N.A. Griswold House (Newport Art Museum), Newport, Rhode Island. Richard Morris Hunt, architect, 1862-63. Operated by Newport Art Museum Open daily except Monday.
79	*National Register*	John J. Glessner House, Chicago, Illinois. H.H. Richardson, architect. 1887. Owned and operated by the Chicago Architecture Foundation. Open daily.
79	*National Register*	Lionberger House, Mid Town Historic District, St. Louis, Missouri. H.H. Richardson, architect. 1886. Privately owned. Not accessible.

Page	Historic Status	Location, Architect, and Accessibility to Public
80	*National Register*	Haas Lilienthal House, San Francisco, California. Peter R. Schmidt, architect. 1880. Owned and operated by the Foundation for San Francisco's Architectural Heritage. Open on limited basis and by appointment.
81	*National Register*	Isaac Bell House (Edna Villa), Newport, Rhode Island. McKim, Mead, and White, architects. 1882-83. Privately owned. Not accessible.
82	*Local Register*	Brewster Apartment Building (Brewster Condominium), Chicago, Illinois. Enoch Hill Turnock, architect. 1893. Privately owned. Not accessible.
84	*National Register*	The Gamble House, Pasadena, California. Greene and Greene, architects. 1908. Owned by the City of Pasadena. Operated by the University of Southern California School of Architecture. Open to the public by appointment for tours.
85	*National Register*	William Gray Warden House, Palm Beach, Florida. Addison Mizner, architect. 1922. Privately owned. Not accessible.
86	*National Register*	J.B. McGay Residence, Gilette Historic District, Tulsa, Oklahoma. John R. Koberling, Jr., architect. 1936. Private residence. Not accessible.
87	*National Register*	Hotel New Yorker, Miami Beach Architectural District, Miami Beach, Florida. Henry Hohauser, architect. 1940. Demolished.
88	*National Register*	The Lovell House (The Health House), Los Angeles, California. Richard Neutra, architect, c. 1927. Privately owned. Not accessible.
101	*National Register*	Bradish-Johnson House (Louise S.McGehee School), Historic Garden District, New Orleans, Louisiana. 1872. Louis E. Reynolds, architect. Owned and operated by the Louise S. McGehee School, Inc. Tours available.

FURTHER READING

America's Architectural Roots: Ethnic Groups That Built America. Washington, D.C.: The Preservation Press, 1986.

Andrews, J.J.C. *The Well-Built Elephant and Roadside Attractions: A Tribute to American Eccentricity*. New York: Congdon and Weed, 1984.

Blumenson, John J. G. *Identifying American Architecture: A Pictorial Guide to Styles and Terms*, 1600 -1945. rev. ed. Nashville, Tenn.: American Association for State and Local History, 1981.

Foley, Mary Mix. *The American House.* New York: Harper and Row, 1980.

Fuller, R. Buckminster, and Robert Marks. *The Dymaxion World of Buckminster Fuller*. New York: Anchor Books, 1973.

Harrison, Henry S. *Houses: The Illustrated Guide to Construction Design and Systems.* Chicago: Realtors National Marketing Institute ® of the National Association of Realtors, 1976.

Kemp, Jim. *American Vernacular: Regional Influences in Architecture and Interior Design.* Washington, D.C.: American Institute of Architects Press, 1987.

Larsen, Michael, and Elizabeth Pomada. *Painted Ladies: San Francisco's Resplendent Victorians*. New York: E.P. Dutton, 1978.

McAlester, Virginia, and Lee McAlester. *A Field Guide to American Houses.* New York: Alfred A. Knopf, 1984.

Maddex, Diane, editor. *Master Builders: A Guide to Famous American Architects.* Washington, D.C.: The Preservation Press, 1985.

News Front/Year, ed. *The Great Innovators.* New York: Year, Inc., 1970.

Poppeliers, John, S. Allen Chambers, and Nancy B. Schwartz. *What Style Is It?* rev. ed. Washington, D.C.: The Preservation Press, 1983.

Rifkin, Carole. *A Field Guide to American Architecture*. New York: New American Library, A Plume Book, 1980.

Schweitzer, Robert, and Michael W.R. Davis. *America's Favorite Homes: Mail Order Catalogues as a Guide to Popular 20th Century Houses*. Detroit: Wayne State University Press, 1990.

Walker, Lester. *American Shelter: An Illustrated Encyclopedia of the American Home.* Woodstock, N.Y.: Overlook Press, 1981.

Whiffen, Marcus. *American Architecture Since 1780: A Guide to the Styles*. Cambridge, Mass.: M.I.T. Press, 1969.

ACKNOWLEDGMENTS

The creation of this book was an exciting and difficult process, involving the help, support, and patience of many individuals. I want to take this opportunity to thank them for their involvement. Should I neglect to mention anyone, please forgive this oversight and know that you, too, are valued.

First and foremost, for her contribution in helping to develop the concept for the book and for invaluable creative input in its early stages, I want to acknowledge and to express my sincere thanks to Ginny Graves, who served as a consultant to this project. Our joint concern about the need for quality architectural education for children has resulted in many collaborations over the years. I do now and will always value her knowledge, insight, and resourcefulness in the field of urban awareness.

The State Historic Preservation Offices, local historical societies, the directors and staffs of historic house museums, and the owners of private homes have been open and receptive in sharing information about their properties with me. In particular, I would like to thank the following individuals for their assistance in my research: Ms. Aimee Helwig, The Foundation for San Francisco‘s Architectural Heritage; Charman A. Adams, Historic Natchez Foundation; Ron Baum, San Antonio Conservation Society; Timothy Samuelson, Commission on Chicago Landmarks; Chere Jiusto, SHPO Montana Historical Society, Helena, Montana; Eileen F. Starr, SHPO Department of Commerce, State of Wyoming, and from that same office Mark Junge and Clayton Frazier for their photographs of Boswell Ranch; Tim Redmond, Planning Manager, City of Carbondale, Illinois, and Bill Perk, Community Development, Southern Illinois University, Carbondale, Illinois, for their help with information on R. Buckminster Fuller; Michael Zimny, Bureau of Historic Preservation, Florida Department of State; Lisa Lassman Bisco, Landmarks Commission, Kansas City, Missouri; Donna Fricker, Division of SHPO Louisiana; John Bonafide, Parks and Recreation and Historic Preservation Field Bureau for New York State; John White, Department of Historic Resources for Virginia; Teresa M. Kinsey, Division of Architecture, Texas Historical Commission, Austin, Texas; Alisha Moore

Stockton, Shoal Creek, Missouri; Susan Mossman, Pasadena Heritage; Ben Kroup, SHPO New York State; Zeb Mayhew, Jr., Oak Alley Plantation, Louisiana; Lori G. Carroll, Cosanti Foundation, Cordes Junction, Arizona; Joan Antonson, Department of Natural Resources Alaska; and Corinne Chun, Friends of `Iolani Palace, Hawaii.

My sincere gratitude to Millard Fuller, president of Habitat for Humanity International, for providing information on this wonderful program and lending his support to this book. Also, a thank you to Crichton Singleton, A.I.A., for introducing me to Mr. Fuller and for his interest in my publication.

A special thank you to Neil Horstmann, executive director of Mount Vernon, for his continued support of my projects while I was a part of his staff at Historic Kansas City Foundation and thereafter. And to my long-time friend Armand Eisen, who more than once took me under his wing and offered good advice and encouragement, my sincere gratitude.

Under Every Roof required me to be in all 50 states – an impossibility, to say the least! I had to rely, therefore, on others who knew the territory and could provide me with names and places to contact. In this area, Ms. Courtney Damkroger, program associate, Western Regional Office of The National Trust for Historic Preservation, was quite resourceful. I am grateful for her efforts on my behalf.

My appreciation to my editors at Preservation Press, Janet Walker and especially Deborah Styles for their thoughtful editing, enthusiasm, and support for this first-time effort. Believing in the project made it happen.

I am indebted to Joe Stites's vision for this book – he has always been able to draw what I am trying to write about. His humor and good nature bailed me out and pushed me forward more than once, from the first draft to the finished product. I was lucky to have had the chance to create this book with him.

Finally, the tremendous encouragement and unfailing interest that my family has shown me from the inception to the completion of *Under Every Roof* must be mentioned here. I am grateful to my first test readers and art critics, my children, Eliot and Ginny. I listened to their comments and made the necessary changes. Thank you for caring so much. For his sage legal advice on all book matters, I am grateful for the counsel of my brother, Tom. My mother assured me that I would find a publisher and that the book would get written, and she reminded me that no matter how large the project, it can only be tackled one piece at a time. Her love and wise advice are reflected in these pages. I want to thank my father for my horse, Louie, who provided me with the riding breaks necessary for me to return refreshed to my writing tasks. And Christopher, my best friend, reader, typist, promoter, crutch, and beloved husband – how could this have been possible without you? This book was a labor of love that I now share with all of you who helped me create it.

PBG